HOW TO
BECOME
A
"FOR REAL"
CHRISTIAN

Jones 7.17-18

HOW TO BECOME

~~A~~

FOR REAL

~~COMFORTABLE~~

CHRISTIAN

Faith, Surrendering

and the Path to

Authentic
~~*Prosperous*~~ *Christianity*

Stephen D. Peterson

HOW TO BECOME A "FOR REAL" CHRISTIAN:
Faith, Surrendering, and the Path to Authentic Christianity

ISBN: 978-1-7338630-0-1 (softcover)
ISBN: 978-1-7338630-1-8 (ebook)
Library of Congress Control Number: 2019903218

Edited by Thomas Womack
Cover design by Tim Green
Interior design and typeset by Katherine Lloyd, The DESK

To Hugh O. Maclellan, Jr.,

a key benefactor of my high school and college,

and an excellent example of godly stewardship

CONTENTS

INTRODUCTION

"I want to be a *for real* Christian!" the woman exclaimed. After years of describing herself as a Christian, she recognized that her life was indistinguishable from the people around her who claimed no faith at all. Despite being relatively prosperous, she struggled with covetousness, fear, and hopelessness. The Bible's promises of joy and peace rang hollow because daily challenges and disappointments drove her to despair: "If I were someone else, I'd say I needed Jesus. But I have Jesus, or at least I thought I did. What's wrong with me?"

Many of us empathize with this woman's frustration. We "prayed to receive Jesus," we attend church, read our Bibles, participate in a small group, and listen to the right podcasts—but our lives remain unchanged. We know something should be different, but we can't identify what's missing. We feel utterly incapable of changing. We claim to have achieved salvation, but our faith has atrophied. We long for a robust, purposeful life of significance, but end up with a "less than" life of daily frustrations and fleeting pleasures.

Is there hope?

Nearly two thousand years ago, James wrote a challenging letter to a group of people struggling to live as "for real" Christians. They were flawed, and they were suffering. James didn't ignore the difficult realities they encountered, but faced them head-on with grace and with truth.

We use the phrase "for real" when we describe something that's authentic as distinguished from something that merely appears so. A for-real baseball fan knows the game, the players on his favorite team, and that team's place in the standings. An inauthentic baseball fan may wear an expensive jersey, but stares at his phone while sitting in corporate box during a playoff game. He's not invested; he's not for real.

If you're living in the western world, you've encountered many professing Christians. Among them are those whose lives are little different from others around them. Others are distinct in their love, their joy, their peace, their patience, and their kindness. When you're in need of wisdom or encouragement, you seek out the people in the latter group. You may not covet their circumstances, but you admire their character. These people are for real.

When I refer to a for-real Christian, I don't mean a perfect Christian. No Christian on earth is perfect. Rather, I'm referring to a Christian whose faith makes an actual difference in life. The for-real Christian makes decisions and reacts to circumstances in ways that are impossible to explain apart from a true belief in things that are not of this earth.

The path to becoming a for-real Christian begins at the cross of Jesus Christ. There's no other way. Jesus himself said so (John 14:6). However, neither this book nor James's letter are primarily concerned with the path to salvation. This book, and James's letter, are for those who've professed belief in Jesus Christ but who struggle with having their faith make a real difference in life.

Here's an uncomfortable truth. The path from salvation to Christian maturity is paved with suffering. Christianity is not merely a moral ethic, a body of wisdom, or a supernatural resource that we add to an otherwise ordinary life. Christianity involves a wholesale surrender to the one who made us and has saved us. Left to our own devices, most of us will continue to live a predictable, pleasure-seeking life. Suffering takes us off that track. It teaches us that the fleeting things of this earth are not what really count. Suffering purifies our hope as Christians.

I'm not glib about suffering. In this fallen world, we don't need to seek suffering, because it comes to all without exception. Almost every day, I read news stories about suffering that seems unfathomable. Sometimes it's happening among people I know and love.

Suffering in itself is not a good thing, and it can produce bitterness as easily as maturity. If we view our suffering only through the prism of this earth, it's an unequivocal evil, entirely unwelcome. Through the prism of eternity, however, suffering can provide us with a proper perspective and deeper faith that will ultimately produce a more enduring joy.

Every reader of this book is suffering in some way. Your suffering may be acute, or it may be the common trials of life we all experience. You may hesitate to describe your circumstances as suffering because you see others enduring far worse. But don't discount your suffering, whatever sort it is. When combined with faithful endurance, it will improve your character and purify your hope.

Despite the universal experience of suffering, we're surprised when it happens to us, and we often despair. Because our lives are full of troubles, we sometimes conclude that there's something wrong with our faith, or maybe with our God. James coaxes us out of our despair by fixing our eyes on eternity.

The Christian walk is not a dour, stoic passage through pain. In fact, God's word tells us that inexpressible joy and great rejoicing are what the path of suffering and faith ultimately leads to. We think suffering is robbing us of the peace we all crave, when in fact it may be the very thing that's pulling us toward it.

Join me for a walk through James's letter, as we consider the path of suffering and faith.

1

JAMES,
BROTHER OF JESUS

James, a bondservant of God and of the Lord Jesus Christ,
to the twelve tribes who are dispersed abroad: Greetings.

JAMES 1:1

The Bible describes the Christian experience as the abundant life (John 10:10). To his disciples, Jesus states his intention for his joy to be in us, and for that joy to be full (John 15:11). He promised his followers an enduring peace (John 14:27). Most of us, however, sense a gap between the Bible's description of the Christian life and the life we're actually living. Instead of joy, we feel despair. Instead of peace, we suffer anxiety.

I'm there often enough. Here's just a fragment of the ample evidence:

My mood has moved in the direction of despair. I can't identify any component of my life that is firing on all cylinders. Work is a slog, my kids are all struggling in some way or another. My wife is wearing the stress of it all on her face. Everything seems bleak.

My personal journal is sprinkled with entries just like that one. They chronicle the times when I experience disconnect between what is and what should be. In those seasons I've often asked, "Can I trust the promises of God's word?"

James wrote his letter to a group of Christians who were suffering. His readers wrestled with the same questions we ask when we suffer. My ambition in this book is that we walk through James's letter much as his original audience did, gleaning eternal truths as applicable today as they were two thousand years ago.

(By the way, don't skip the Bible passages from James that I quote at the beginning of each chapter. These, as well as other Scripture quotations, are the only words on the pages of this book that I can say are absolutely true. Read each passage slowly and with particular care. My words will pass away, but God's words endure forever.)

We learn a great deal about this letter's author and audience in its first sentence. We learn that the author is a man named James. This James (as we learn elsewhere, in Mark 6:3 and Galatians 1:19), was the half-brother of Jesus. However, James didn't initially believe his brother Jesus was the Son of God. In fact, he and his siblings for a time thought Jesus was crazy (Mark 3:21). The apostle John writes, "Not even Jesus's brothers were believing him" (John 7:5). As far as we know, James persisted in that unbelief throughout Jesus's life.

So what happened to the skeptic James between Christ's death and James's writing of this powerful epistle? What happened is that James encountered the risen Christ.

The apostle Paul writes that James was one of the people to whom Christ appeared individually after his resurrection (1 Corinthians 15:7). James knew his brother had died—then saw him alive. This encounter with the resurrected Jesus brought a monumental change in James, and he went on to become a leader of the church in Jerusalem (Acts 12:17; 15:13; Galatians 2:9). Information given by the historian Josephus indicates that James was martyred for his faith in A.D. 62.[1] James, who'd interacted daily with Jesus for most of his life, and who initially rejected him as the promised Messiah, ultimately gave up his life because of his belief that this same man was the Son of God.

We also learn something about James's character from this first sentence of his letter. With all the qualifications James could have used to describe himself—half-brother of Jesus, someone to whom the risen Christ appeared, head of the church in Jerusalem—he chose instead to describe himself as the "bondservant" of God and of Christ. The original word here is *doulos*, a Greek term used throughout the New Testament for "slave." That voluntary designation on James's part brings to mind an interesting stipulation from Old Testament law. The law mandated that a Hebrew holding another Hebrew as a slave was to release that slave after six years of service (Exodus 21:2), but a slave who loved his master was allowed to voluntarily subject himself to that master for the rest of his life (21:5). James was proclaiming himself to be a willing slave and bondservant of God and of the Lord Jesus Christ; he wanted to be known because of the master he served, not for any personal marker of status.

From this letter's opening words we also learn about James's audience. The "twelve tribes" is a reference to Jewish Christians dispersed from Jerusalem because of persecution under Herod Agrippa (we'll learn more about that later). Some scholars date James's letter just after this dispersion—at some point between A.D. 45 and 50, making it the first New Testament book to be written.[2]

James's transformation from skeptic to follower was a result of his encounter with the resurrected Christ. The spiritual journey of all for-real Christians must begin in the same place, with a belief in the resurrected Jesus. But James's journey didn't end with mere belief, and neither will ours, if we're to grow into a mature faith. The mature insight James demonstrates in his letter is the fruit of faithful endurance through suffering.

We all suffer. Our suffering might take the common forms of job stress, marital tension, and parental exhaustion. It may include the more acute pain of terminal illness, the loss of a child, or a divorce. All this suffering, whether common or acute, can produce either growth or bitterness. If we measure our lives by our comfort during the span of our years on this earth, then any suffering is likely to produce resentment. If we view our lives as the brief period of time that we can invest toward eternity, then we can receive suffering with joy, because God can use suffering to purify our hope.

James provides us with a lens through which we can endure our suffering with peace as we grow toward maturity. With this lens, the trials we so desperately hope to avoid can become the very things that produce the joy, peace, and significance we so often lack.

Discussion Questions:

1. While James could have described himself as "leader of the church in Jerusalem" or "half-brother of Jesus," he instead refers to himself simply as the bondservant of Jesus. Why do you imagine James did that?

2. Why do you think we're sometimes tempted to let people know about our own spiritual résumés or accomplishments for God?

3. Does the topic of suffering repel you, or interest you? Are you suffering now?

2

JOY IN TRIALS

Consider it all joy, my brethren,
when you encounter various trials,
knowing that the testing of your faith produces endurance.
And let endurance have its perfect result,
so that you may be perfect and complete, lacking in nothing....
Blessed is the man who perseveres under trial;
for once he has been approved, he will receive the crown of life
which the Lord has promised to those who love him.

JAMES 1:2-4,12

The twelfth chapter of Acts describes a horrible persecution of Jewish Christians instituted by Herod Agrippa in approximately A.D. 44. Herod was Rome's puppet king over Jerusalem. In a vicious response to the Christian faith, which continued to grow despite prior persecutions, Herod executed a man named James (not our author, but rather one of Jesus's original twelve disciples). This execution pleased the unbelieving Jews, so Herod arrested Peter, who seemed certain to die also. After Peter's arrest, the Christian Jews in Jerusalem were in hiding, praying for Peter's deliverance and for their own protection. God miraculously delivered Peter from prison, but persecution in Jerusalem

9

continued, forcing Jewish Christians to flee Jerusalem and settle in other areas of the Roman Empire. These scattered refugees from religious persecution were the recipients of James's letter.

It's difficult for most of us to imagine a trial as severe as the threat of arrest and execution. New Christians in Jerusalem were anticipating the victorious return of Christ, but instead they suffered persecution and witnessed the execution of their friend and leader. Other refugees had fled earlier because of the stoning of Stephen, Christianity's first martyr. It was in regard to these circumstances that James wrote, "Consider it all joy."

While Christians all over the globe are today suffering trials very similar to those endured by the first generation church, most people reading this book are suffering trials of a different sort. Christians often expect lives full of victorious circumstances and instead suffer things like illness, divorce, job loss, rebellious children, fear, and stress. Are we to consider all this joy? Yes. The Greek word in James 1:2 translated as "all" means both "every" and "all."[3]

If God loves us, and we seek him, why do these trials come? And when they do, how are we to respond?

Many philosophies and religious systems value suffering and even seek it. But the Christian view of suffering is different. James isn't calling us to a state of resigned detachment, as taught by stoics; nor is he extolling the inherent goodness of difficult trials, like some masochist. Nor are trials valuable only because they toughen us up for harder trials to come. Rather, the Christian can experience joy in trials because those trials are accomplishing in us an ultimate and more significant end, which James defines for us here: to be perfect and complete in Christ.

In whatever form our trials take, they test our faith. Such testing can result in either bitterness or a joyful endurance.

In emphasizing the importance of endurance for the Christian, James wasn't alone among the New Testament writers. Paul writes,

> Therefore, having been justified by faith, we have peace with God through our Lord Jesus Christ, through whom also we have obtained our introduction by faith into this grace in which we stand; and we exult in hope of the glory of God. And not only this, but we also exult in our tribulations, knowing that tribulation brings about perseverance; and perseverance, proven character; and proven character, hope; and hope does not disappoint, because the love of God has been poured out within our hearts through the Holy Spirit who was given to us. (Romans 15:1-5)

Paul here outlines our path to joyous Christian living. First, we rejoice in the position we've attained before God, because God has given us an eternal, glorious inheritance through his grace. Then we celebrate our inevitable tribulations because these develop endurance, which proves character, which brings about hope—and hope does not disappoint. This is not a hope in changed circumstances, because circumstances may not change. Yet the hope to which we're called is a hope for the here and now, and seeking fulfillment in intimacy with God. This hope for intimacy with God is partially realized now on this earth and will be fully realized in heaven, when:

> He will wipe every tear from their eyes. There will be no more death or mourning or crying or pain, for the old order of things has passed away. (Revelation 21:4)

Our perseverance in tribulation strips away the earthly things from which we derive temporary comfort and false peace, and it directs us to the source of true sustenance and eternal peace. Enduring through tribulation separates us from the false and unites us with the true.

Peter joins Paul and James in exhorting us to endure and rejoice in our trials, pointing us to the greater goal:

> In this you greatly rejoice even though now for a little while, if necessary, you have been distressed by various trials, so that the proof of your faith, being more precious than gold which is perishable, even though tested by fire, may be found to result in praise and glory and honor at the revelation of Jesus Christ; and though you have not seen him, you love him, and though you do not see him now, but believe in him, you greatly rejoice with joy inexpressible and full of glory, obtaining as the outcome of your faith the salvation of your souls. (1 Peter 1:6-9)

Great rejoicing? Inexpressible joy? Even in our most pleasant circumstances these things can be elusive, and yet these writers say we can rejoice and experience joy in the midst of great tribulation. The reason we don't experience great rejoicing and inexpressible joy is that we expect our idols (money, weight loss, beauty, new homes, possessions, professional promotion, successful children, etc.) to deliver us enduring joy, and they can't. Sometimes, in the very moment when we get the thing we want, we experience a nagging disappointment instead of great rejoicing. This is because we've burdened that thing with the weight of delivering ultimate joy. Ironically, when we're seeking joy in God and rejoicing in intimacy with him, we experience greater pleasure in things like relationships, cars, houses, and vacations because we haven't burdened those finite and imperfect things with delivering the unending joy we crave.

Whenever we expect something other than God to deliver joy, peace, or security, that thing is an idol to us. God is constantly working to purge us of our idolatry.

The greatest idol in my life has been professional success, and God has been working to remove that idol for my entire adult life. I was a dedicated, professing Christian when I entered law school, but I soon became enamored with thoughts of money and power. In God's mercy, he didn't allow me any attractive job opportunities upon graduation. I took the very unusual path of starting my own law firm with a classmate.

For nearly four years, I struggled to get clients and stumbled through learning the law while my student loans accrued interest. I drove an old hatchback without air conditioning (in Atlanta no less), risked life without health insurance, and rarely knew from one month to the next how I would pay my rent. I directed all my energy and prayers and hope toward improved circumstances in the form of professional success. Though God consistently provided a roof over my head and food for my table, he delayed giving me the success I craved because he had higher intentions for me. God wanted to remove my idol so I could learn that God is good and that God is enough. The path for me from idolatry to joyful dependence on God has been paved with suffering—because there's no other path.

James writes (in 1:12) that the man who perseveres under trial will receive the crown of life. The Greek word translated here as "crown" was used for the wreath placed on the head of a victorious athlete or military leader in the ancient world.[4] Athletes and generals endure and sacrifice a great deal on their way to success. A lot of that suffering is unseen, anonymous, grinding, and inglorious in the moment. But the one who succeeds will endure such suffering by keeping his eyes fixed on the end result, the crown. On the pedestal, when the great king places the crown on the head of the victor, the suffering pales.

Paul, Peter, and James all point us toward a perfect result. They're not asking us to enjoy trials for the trials' sake, nor do they exhort us to endure for the sake of enduring. They're pointing us ultimately toward the result of endurance—which is our becoming perfect and entire, lacking in nothing. The Greek word translated in James 1:4 as "perfect" is *teleios,* and refers not to moral perfection but to completed growth—a mature adult as opposed to a child.[5] The word translated there as "complete" is *holokleros*—meaning "having all its parts."[6] Paul, Peter, and James urge us to endure trials so that we'll become mature and whole.

We often feel the opposite of this. We feel underdeveloped, less than whole, as if we're missing some parts. Do you want to change this? Do you desire to be mature, in possession of "all your parts," and living a resiliently joyful life? Then reframe your view of the suffering in your life. Ease and comfort do not produce maturity and resilient peace. These things come only through faithful endurance in trials. The Bible doesn't call us to seek trials, but when they come, welcome them as friends, and let endurance achieve its perfect result.

Discussion Questions

1. As you think back about a particular trial you've experienced in life, how did you feel about it when you first encountered it?
2. What's the correlation between knowing God's character and being able to walk positively through trials?

3. It's been said that most American Christians pray for God to get them out of the trials they face, whereas the rest of the world's Christians pray for God to get them *through* their trials. What does James 1:2-4 have to say about these two different perspectives?

3

ON WISDOM AND ASKING GOD

But if any of you lacks wisdom, let him ask of God,
who gives to all generously and without reproach, and it will
be given to him. But he must ask in faith without any doubting,
for the one who doubts is like the surf of the sea, driven and
tossed by the wind. For that man ought not to expect that he
will receive anything from the Lord, being a
double-minded man, unstable in all his ways.

JAMES 1:5-8

Some time ago, my family needed a car. Our need was legitimate, but I really wanted a luxury label car, which was less legitimate. Despite my early lessons in humility, I felt the increasing need to drive a car that matched my perceived status as a partner in a large law firm. In other words, I wanted my car to project success. In the spirit of good stewardship, I was still willing to buy a used car. (See how spiritual I am?) And my wife and I had previously decided to avoid incurring any more debt than we already had, so we were limited to the amount of money we'd already set aside for a new car.

Claiming the very passage from James quoted above, I asked God for wisdom about buying another car. Just in case God was unaware, I also told him that a particular Lexus was the highest rated used car available. (I'm often helpful to God in that way.)

I had a good friend who'd just bought a new car and still had his old one. Shortly after buying the new car, he went through a job transition and needed to sell his old car, which had all the features I needed. It had low mileage and good fuel efficiency, had been well maintained, and featured all the bells and whistles I'd hoped for in a car. Importantly, my friend was selling it for the exact amount of money I'd set aside. But the car lacked one feature. It wasn't a luxury label car.

God had given me wisdom, and the opportunity to act on that wisdom. The question now was whether I would apply it.

As I wrestled and prayed about the car, it became clear to me that the car wasn't the issue. In the broader perspective, I was frustrated that my life didn't match the image I wanted to project with the car. I was frustrated that the Giver of all good gifts hadn't seen fit to give me more, though he'd given me much.

I don't profess to hear the audible voice of God, but at times I do have conversations with God in my head. I cried out, "God, why are these things so hard? Why can't I have some of the things that so many other people have? What have I done wrong? Why are you constantly disciplining me?" And God replied, "What have I not given you? All your needs are met, and now you have the opportunity to buy exactly the car you need, incurring no debt and helping a friend in the process. The one thing you lack is the one thing I don't want you to have—worldly prestige."

I'd be dishonest if I said my submission was 100 percent joyful. But I obeyed, and I've been blessed in that obedience. Did

God honor my request for wisdom? Yes, but on a higher level than where I was asking him to operate.

God is constantly disciplining me because he disciplines everyone he loves as his child (Hebrews 12:6). And the wisdom he gave me allowed me to address something of far greater significance than my need for a car.

Your own current struggle may be far more painful and confusing than the one I just described. (I have those too.) But remember that God's response to your repeated requests may well be on an altogether higher level than the one on which you're expecting him to operate.

This passage in James begins with a qualifier: "If any of you lacks wisdom..." I imagine that everyone reading this book falls into that category. That's not a comment on the character of my readers, but on the rarity of genuine wisdom. James goes on to give an encouraging promise: Wisdom from God is readily available if we ask for it. But that promise is balanced with a warning. We can't expect to receive the wisdom we ask for if our motivations are double-minded.

In considering this passage, we should define wisdom. The Greek word is *sophia*. Scholars define the term in various ways: as "insight into the true nature of things";[7] "the understanding and practical skill that's necessary to live life to God's glory; not a wisdom of philosophical speculation, but the wisdom contained in the pure and peaceable absolutes of God's will revealed in his word and lived out";[8] and "the knowledge of how to regulate one's relationship with God."[9]

Wisdom is best understood as the practical application of God's word and his truths to the circumstances of our lives. Wisdom is not equivalent to knowledge. If it were, James would have written, "If any of you lacks wisdom, he should study." Wisdom is the ability to apply God's truth to the challenges we face. Wisdom is a divine gift.

King Solomon is the most famous wise man in Scripture. His early adulthood was defined by wisdom. Given an opportunity to ask God for anything he wanted, Solomon didn't ask for wealth, power, or fame, but for wisdom (1 Kings 3:3-14). God was so pleased with this request that he granted Solomon not only wisdom but also things he didn't request—riches and honor. This says something about Solomon but also about God: God gives lavishly to his children, and he esteems wisdom. (Later in Solomon's life, he forsook wisdom; he ceased applying God's truths to every circumstance of his life, and he lapsed into unrighteousness and despair.)

James tells us that if we ask for wisdom, we (like Solomon) will receive it from God, because God gives to all generously and without reproach. Yet many of us have asked God for good things that we didn't receive.

Note, however, that this particular passage is limited to requests for wisdom. That's not to say God doesn't also give lavishly and without reproach in other contexts, but this particular passage doesn't address other sorts of requests. We must also consider that James is writing to people who are suffering trials of many kinds, and he's encouraging them to rejoice in their humble circumstances. These sufferers almost certainly prayed to God for relief from their persecution and for deliverance from their humbling circumstances, and yet what's promised here is not a change in circumstances but an increase in wisdom.

You see, wisdom is essential if we're to rejoice in suffering, because only wisdom will allow us to see God's working even in our trials. Only wisdom recognizes the spiritual value of living in humbling circumstances. Worldly wisdom, which James discusses more fully in chapter 3, doesn't see the value in these things. Worldly wisdom seeks comfort, and considers all suffering to be evil.

We get spiritually discouraged when we confuse wisdom with things like wealth and self-fulfillment. We pretend we're seeking godly wisdom when in fact we want God to do *our* will, to equip us with helpful insight for obtaining wealth, or to help us manipulate things so we can get our own *way*. Too often we think of wisdom as some special advantage God can give us at work or elsewhere, some decision-making ability that will provide us with more pleasant and prosperous circumstances. We can dress all this up as "wisdom," but it's really something else. The wisdom promised in James involves another sphere of God's working, one that's more likely to change our character than our circumstances.

James wasn't promising his readers the wisdom to engineer better circumstances, but the wisdom to more clearly see and experience God's working in their lives. Too often we try to harness God's power to our own ends, and he'll never serve in that role. He's always working to bring us to greater dependence on him and submission to him, because that's where we find greater joy in him. We must understand wisdom in that context.

This passage suggests to some that we'll get wisdom only if we're absolutely certain God will give it to us. This makes for a frustratingly conditional promise, because our degree of certainty can easily waver, especially in the midst of a trial. But the passage is really saying something else. Thomas Constable of Dallas Theological Seminary specifically identifies the NASB translation (which I use here) as "unfortunate." According to Constable, the passage more accurately reads, "Let him ask in faith, free from divided motives and divisive attitudes."[10] It's not a matter of asking God for something with the emotional certainty that God will deliver, but a matter of asking God for wisdom with the intention of serving him by applying that wisdom when God gives it.

As James discusses later in his letter, faith is evidenced by action. We evidence belief when we act on the wisdom God provides. The double-minded man is one who pretends to seek God's wisdom when in fact he's seeking his own will. He seeks God's wisdom only as an alternative to be weighed against other options. This was Solomon's folly in his later life—he didn't become less intelligent, but he stopped being obedient, and in that disobedience he evidenced a loss of faith. The fruit of that folly was discouragement and despair.

James likens the double-minded man to the sea's waves. Water forms in waves when it's acted upon by external forces, and it moves completely at the whim of those forces. The double-minded man has placed one foot each in two competing systems—the system of the world and the kingdom of God. Those systems are incompatible. Like someone straddling two boats on a choppy sea, the double-minded man is unstable. He'll accomplish nothing of enduring significance. Those who seeks to direct and control their own life rather than surrendering that control completely to God will spend their life tossed by the waves of circumstances. They receive neither the peace that passes understanding nor enduring joy. They don't experience the life which is "life indeed" (1 Timothy 6:19). Yet they probably ask God why they're not receiving joy and peace. Here's God's answer: "Because you're double-minded; your requests for wisdom are self-serving, rather than prioritizing the God you pretend to serve."

The goal of true wisdom is not trial avoidance. If we view wisdom that way, we miss the point. The wisdom promised here allows us to faithfully endure our trials, to make good decisions in the midst of trial, and to see God at work in our difficulties. This wisdom leads to the peace of knowing that our trials are never outside God's sovereign design, and that his design is good.

Discussion Questions

1. Most of us have asked for wisdom at some point in our lives. Think of a time when you've made such a request. Were you seeking something other than the kind of wisdom James teaches us about? If so, what were you really seeking?

2. How would you compare the kind of wisdom James describes in this passage with any concept of wisdom you've previously held? Which kind of wisdom is more attractive to you, and why?

3. Are there particular areas in your life where you struggle with double-mindedness—trying to mix the world's wisdom with God's wisdom? What do you think are the reasons for this struggle?

4

INSIDE THE UPSIDE DOWN KINGDOM

But the brother of humble circumstances is to glory in
his high position; and the rich man is to glory in his humiliation,
because like flowering grass he will pass away.
For the sun rises with a scorching wind and withers the grass;
and its flower falls off and the beauty of its appearance is destroyed;
so too the rich man in the midst of his pursuits will fade away.

JAMES 1:9-11

In my journal, I sometimes create a "worry list." I do that to identify where I need to confess, where idols are showing their presence, and where I need God to provide. As I pull old journals off the shelf, I'm often encouraged to see the many ways in which God has answered my prayers. What's less encouraging is the persistence of my worries related to money. I frequently inventory what I have and what I need, fretting at the perceived gap. Rather than rejoicing in the abundance God has provided, I envy those who seem to have more. Worry and covetousness erode my joy, extinguish my peace, and inhibit my capacity to love others.

I speak with enough people to know that my struggle isn't unusual. For all who struggle to maintain a healthy relationship with money, James's words in 1:9-11 serve to both challenge and encourage.

Scripture is full of encouraging promises to the poor and cautions to the rich. The prophets spoke of a coming liberation of the poor and oppressed (Malachi 3:5; Isaiah 58:6-7; 61:1). Luke quotes Jesus as saying, "Blessed are you who are poor, for yours is the kingdom of God," and, "Woe to you who are rich, for you are receiving your comfort in full" (Luke 6:20,24). James himself will elaborate further on the perils of wealth later in his letter.

For most of the people hearing these words in the thousands of years since they were written, these passages have been a source of tremendous encouragement and hope. But we of the prosperous western world hear these words and think, "Uh oh, what does this mean for me?" Most of us still covet money because we still believe that money, rather than God, will meet our core needs.

Many modern teachers comfort the rich in light of the Bible's teaching about money, trying to explain why the wealthy are off the hook. But we can't escape the hook so easily. If our reflexive response to a warning is to assume it doesn't apply to us, we're putting ourselves in peril.

These warnings in Scripture are not a lash to punish the rich, but a compassionate warning designed to keep us from shallow lives of futility. We Christians serve an upside down kingdom. The things valued in this eternal kingdom are not what's valued in this temporary world. In fact, the values of Christ's kingdom and the values of this world stand in opposition to each other. Yet we Christians often measure the quality of our lives and the goodness of our God by the degree to which our present circumstances measure up to worldly values. The more comfortable we are by those standards, the easier it is to serve the idol of material prosperity. When we desire comfort more than we desire God, we sentence ourselves to a shallow spiritual relationship, never really going deep in intimacy with God.

It's challenging, and often disorienting, to live inside this upside down kingdom because the voices from the false kingdom are so loud and strident. We must displace these seductive voices with the word of God. Our trials are useful because they serve to highlight the enduring value of God's kingdom, while unveiling the world's false values that oppose it. Trials often reveal what needs to pass away in our lives.

"The brother" mentioned in James 1:9 refers to a believer in Christ. James is writing to Jewish members of the Christian church who were formerly in Judea and had been dispersed around the known world. Among these believers were both poor and rich. The trials they were enduring lowered the earthly status of both the poor and the rich. James's words are intended to comfort them both.

James tells the believer in humble circumstances to glory in his high position. The Greek word *tapeinos*, translated by the phrase "of humble circumstances," literally means "of low degree."[11] The word in that verse translated as "glory" refers to boasting about a privilege or possession.[12] James's exhortation to glory in humility is not sarcastic. He was telling these brothers in humble circumstances to rejoice in their present physical lack because of a certain future reality.

The believer who's poor in the things of this earth can rejoice that his current estate doesn't define his eternity, and that he has a glorious future. The poor man doesn't have to pass through the eye of a needle to enter the kingdom of God because he hasn't been seduced into thinking he's already arrived.

In a similar way, Paul linked present suffering with future glory when he described believers as "fellow heirs with Christ, if indeed we suffer with him so that we may also be glorified with him. For I consider that the sufferings of this present time are not worthy to be compared with the glory that is to be revealed to us" (Romans 8:17-18). Peter encouraged his readers not to focus on their current earthly trials, but pointed them instead to "an inheritance which is imperishable and undefiled and will not fade away, reserved in heaven for you" (1 Peter 1:4).

James (in 1:10) adds that when the rich man encounters a lowering of his status, he too can "glory"; he can rejoice in his humiliation, because God is using that trial to purify this faith.

Not many of us think of ourselves as wealthy, but in any historical or global sense, most people reading this book are rich. Perhaps you're suffering financial anxiety, but very few of us in our culture have legitimate worries about having something to eat today or a place to sleep tonight. Most of our concerns are several tomorrows removed from today. Our greatest peril is not the possibility of starving; it's that we might buy the lie that accumulating more money is the antidote to our fears. Since material prosperity appears within reach, and people around us seem to have obtained it, we naturally place our hope in our money, our skills, our networks, or other resources for meeting our needs. Unlike the genuinely poor person, when we're faced with trials, we don't seek God with an expectation of deliverance; instead we look to our physical resources to meet the need. Our prayers are often just a hedge in case other resources fail. Prayer is a last resort rather than a constant discipline. We don't really believe in the power of God to provide.

I'll describe two men and ask you whose life more closely matches the life God wants for us. The first man doesn't know how he's going to meet next month's needs, yet he never lacks for life's essentials because he regularly experiences God's miraculous provision. God and his promises are not abstractions for this man because he depends on them for his daily bread. He constantly and naturally speaks of God's working in his life because that's his reality. Having directly and regularly experienced God's deliverance and provision, he's spiritually mature, and his faith is strong. When the next trial comes, he doesn't shrink in dread but sees another opportunity for a miracle. He's joyful and looks forward to the kingdom to come, because the idea that what's best is what's here holds no temptation for him.

The next man, another brother in Christ, is rich in the things of this earth. He's esteemed in his profession, he has enjoyed a good income, he has fully funded his retirement, and he has set aside money to provide a nice start for his kids. But he still worries. Global events constantly threaten another market disruption. New competitive threats and regulatory changes regularly arise in his work. He has experienced some trials and was able to address them with money, but he frets because he had to draw down his reserves. He lives in dread of the next trial because he's unsure whether his accounts can withstand another crisis. He prays about those things, but so far he's had the resources to handle his trials, and he finds it difficult to trust God fully. For him, it's not enough that God has promised to provide; he needs to know how and when God will do it. Sometimes he wonders if God exists at all. He's healthy and handsome, but the years take their toll; he sees friends get sick, and he worries that his own life might get cut short. He spends a lot of time worrying about losing what he has, but not much time looking forward to the kingdom to come.

Which of these men's lives more closely matches what God intends?

And now a more difficult question: Which of these lives would you rather live?

James wasn't just challenging the rich; he was encouraging them. These rich brothers who were suffering hardship were to rejoice in their humiliation—their being brought low. Again, this is not sarcastic or punitive. James wants these brothers to rejoice in their humiliation because that humiliation serves to purify their hope and reorder their priorities—it forces them into a position of dependence on God.

James 1:11 is a warning to the rich, and one we can't ignore. Grass in the arid Mediterranean area turns green and lush for a brief season, until harsh winds come and dry it out.[13] It flowers for a season, then passes away. So too the rich man. In the midst of his pursuits, he'll fade away. It's not his pursuits that will fade away, but the man himself. Tim Kizziar has said, "Our greatest fear as individuals and as a church should not be of failure, but of succeeding at things in life that don't really matter."[14] Are we so engaged in our drive to acquire and store up that we miss the only relationship that will endure for eternity? Would we rather have a resource-rich life and a tepid relationship with God, or a life of constant dependence on God and a resulting rich intimacy with Jesus?

Heat purifies precious metals by forcing the dross to the surface, where it can be taken off. Trials purify us by forcing to the surface our lack of faith, our character flaws, and our false priorities, allowing us to identify, confess, and purge. What's left is more refined, more useful, more pure. Those truly wise and lovely people in your life—the ones you seek out in the midst of your own trials—are not generally the wealthiest, but those who've been seasoned by faithful endurance through trial.

I once had a conversation with a woman who was hosting me in her vacation home. It was an elegant spot overlooking the ocean. She was a delightful churchgoing woman who'd raised her children to love the Lord. I was telling her about my parents who'd decided to take early retirement to go on the mission field. I told her how joyful and excited my parents were, what a great opportunity they'd been presented, and how proud I was of their choices. As I was telling her this very positive story, her face betrayed distress. She looked horrified. She finally said, "Oh, I hope God never asks me to do that! I love this place too much."

The only difference between this woman and most of us is that she was candid. Most of us have achieved a level of comfort we don't want to surrender. We've become servants of a false kingdom and forfeited the joy and peace that come from serving the True One.

Many of us struggle with a disconnect between God's promise of joy and the lack of joy in our lives. Instead of joyful, we feel unfruitful and beset with stress. The reason we fail to be fruitful is that we're like the thorny soil Jesus spoke of: "And others are the ones on whom seed was sown among the thorns; these are the ones who have heard the word, but the worries of the world and the deceitfulness of riches and the desires for other things enter in and choke the word and it becomes unfruitful" (Mark 4:18-19).

When we experience challenging circumstances, we who are rich should glory in being brought low, because those very humiliations are removing the thorns that prevent fruitfulness. In faithful endurance, we'll know the joy of abiding in Christ, and our lives will begin producing the love, joy, peace, patience, and kindness that a for-real Christian displays.

Discussion Questions

1. These verses in James 1:9-11 are meant not only to warn the rich, but also to encourage them. How were you encouraged?

2. It has been said, "Show me your budget and I'll show you what you love." Considering that we cannot serve both God and the things of this world, what are some principles from this passage that may impact how we set personal or family financial goals?

3. We should all rejoice that God uses trials to purge the Mark 4 "thorns" from our life. What can we do in the midst of prosperity to ensure that we're relying upon the Lord and honoring him with our lives? And how does the concept of sacrificial giving play into this scenario?

5

SIN'S
CYCLE OF DEATH

Blessed is the man who perseveres under trial; for once he has
been approved, he will receive the crown of life which the Lord
has promised to those who love him. Let no one say when he is
tempted, "I am being tempted by God"; for God cannot
be tempted by evil and he himself does not tempt anyone.
But each one is tempted when he is carried away and enticed by
his own lust. Then when lust has conceived, it gives birth to sin;
and when sin is accomplished, it brings forth death.

JAMES 1:12-15

All of us sin, and as Christians we know our sins are forgiven. But we too easily surrender to the idea that our repeated patterns of sin are inevitable, as if there's no way out. We act and think as if we're still enslaved.

It's a mindset that ignores Scripture's repeated promises of freedom for the Christian. For Paul tells us, "Now that you have been set free from sin and have become slaves to God, the benefit you reap leads to holiness, and the result is eternal life" (Romans 6:22). And also: "For the law of the Spirit of life in Christ Jesus has set you free from the law of sin and death" (Romans 8:2). Our lives often don't feel this way, however, so we sometimes question the reality of these promises. We experience repeated patterns of sin with either glib resignation or hopeless despair.

James describes for us (in 1:12-15) sin's cycle of death—the process that allows sin to be conceived in us, to be born, and ultimately to bring death. In describing this cycle, James equips us to avoid the trap.

The process of sin begins with our own lust. To "lust" is the desire to do, have, or be something apart from the will of God. The Greek word translated in 1:14 as "carried away" was a reference to a baited trap for wild game. In the same verse, the word translated as "enticed" was a fishing term, referring to a baited hook or net.[15] We want things that are not of God, and this desire carries us away to a dangerous place. In that dangerous place, we see the appealing bait that hides the fisherman's hook or lures us into the hunter's trap, as we forget the fisherman or hunter's intent. That's why Peter reminds us, "Be of sober spirit, be on the alert. Your adversary, the devil, prowls around like a roaring lion, seeking someone to devour" (1 Peter 5:8).

Two of the most notable biblical examples of sin are the first sin in the garden of Eden, and the sin of David with Bathsheba. Let's look at them both.

In Genesis 3 we read that Eve's sin began with desire stimulated by a lie. Satan approached her in the form of a serpent and asked, "Did God really say you can't eat from the trees of the garden?" She responded, "We can eat of any tree, but one." The serpent lied again: "You will surely not die, and in fact God has prohibited your eating from that tree only because he knows your eyes will be opened, and you'll be like God."

In the face of temptation, we often ask, "Did God really say...?"

The question plants doubt and creates an opening for a lie. The lie is that the prohibited thing is actually a good thing to get, and that a stingy God is keeping us from it.

Eve listened to that lie, and the baited trap was set to spring. She considered this tree and its fruit, rather than fleeing from the scene and from the tempter. She saw that the fruitful tree was good for food, a delight to the eyes, and desirable to make one wise. She took from the tree's fruit and ate. Eve should have avoided that tree; instead she reached for its fruit. I can imagine her touching, fondling, twisting it to get a better view—then it detached from the tree. Taking a bite was now almost inevitable.

What was the consequence? Not life, not joy, not peace, but the greatest tragedy in history—death came into the world.

With each sin of our own, we repeat that pattern and experience the same result, which is death.

What is your forbidden fruit? Do you fix your mind on something that's outside God's will for you? Rather than fleeing, do you expose yourself to this thing over and over—touching it, considering it? Do you find yourself asking, "Did God really say…?" Did God really say I'm supposed to submit to my husband? Did God really say I'm not supposed to gossip? Did God really say I'm not supposed to covet? Is your forbidden fruit the desire to be desired, the ambition to be envied, the craving of people's approval more than God's? The consequence of these sins is death—death of the working of the Holy Spirit in our lives, death of our integrity, death of our witness, and death of our joy.

In 2 Samuel 11 we find David at his palace when he should have been at war. The great warrior king sent his men out to fight while he stayed home. What desires prompted David to do this? We can only speculate—but it's not a stretch to think he was tired of fighting, he wanted rest, he wanted leisure, he wanted entertainment. It's a common default mode of men—resting when we should be working. Then, in 2 Samuel 11:2, the baited hook is presented. David saw Bathsheba, beautiful in appearance, bathing on her roof. He called for her, he slept with her, and she became pregnant.

Rather than confessing and repenting at any point in this cycle, David compounded his sin by killing her husband. The fruit of this sin was not joy, or satisfaction, or peace—but death. The narrative in 2 Samuel includes the physical death of Uriah (Bathsheba's husband) and of the child who was conceived. It also describes the death of David's character and witness. For all the great reasons to remember David, we also remember him for his great sin.

Sin never delivers what it promises. It always delivers death.

David and Bathsheba later had another son, Solomon, who became the wisest man in the world. Solomon later wrote, "What has been will be again, what has been done will be done again; there is nothing new under the sun" (Ecclesiastes 1:9). Some three thousand years after King David's great sin, men are still carried away by the enticement of beautiful naked women. This enticement has never been more pervasive or more easily realized than it is today. In a private moment with a computer, tablet, or smart phone, a man can access any imaginable image. The baited hook hangs constantly in front of us. Many of us have bitten that hook, and are steadily progressing toward death. We lie—to ourselves, to our friends, to our wives. And the result is death—death of our integrity, death of the healthy sexuality God intends for us, and death of our relationships.

Men live isolated in these dark waters, staring incessantly at the bait—knowing it hides a hook, but feeling powerless to do anything other than bite. Shame compounds, and we stay enslaved in the darkness.

I'm not immune to this temptation or to this sin. But I also know that liberation from slavery to sin is available. I know it because God's word promises us freedom from sin, and I know it because I've experienced it. The step from slavery to freedom is a painful one, but it's not obscure. As James writes later in his letter, we're to confess our sins to one another so we may be healed. We're to confess not just silently in prayer to God, but to one another—to the people we've sinned against. And we must repent, which isn't merely to feel remorse, but to turn in the other direction. Satan's aim is to keep us in the dark, continuing in sin and shame, never bringing it into the light, and remaining ineffective and unfruitful. God's alternative to this bleak scenario is that we bring our sin into the light by confessing. The for-real Christian lives a life of transparency, confession, and repentance, rather than shame, lies, and hiding.

James begins his discussion about sin by saying that these temptations do not come from God. One lie that we believe in the midst of temptation is that God wants something for us when his word says otherwise. We say to ourselves, "Well, God gave me a longing to be cherished, and my husband ignores me, so how can it be a sin to seek the attention of men other than my husband?" Or, "God gave me a strong sex drive that my wife won't satisfy, so how can it be wrong for me to seek fulfillment of that drive somewhere else?" The lie is along these lines: "God wants me to be happy." When the bait hangs in front of us, we convince ourselves it must be of God or it wouldn't be there (since he's sovereign after all). James blunts this lie, stating clearly that we can never claim that God is the author of these temptations. God isn't the one setting the trap or baiting the hook; it's our own desires leading us astray. God intends other things for us—far better things that bring life rather than death.

Grave sin rarely comes about as a spontaneous reaction, but results from a series of choices. We make decisions every day that either take us toward sin or away from it. We need to identify where we are in this death cycle of sin and interrupt it before it reaches the inevitable result. We interrupt that cycle by reading Scripture (which defines sin), by confessing our sin to those we've sinned against, and by repenting from that sin by changing our heart and our behavior.

The ultimate reward for endurance in the face of temptation is "the crown of life" (James 1:12), which is an eternal reward. But the rewards begin earlier, as we experience the reconciliation of relationships and the freedom from sin that comes from righteousness, confession, and repentance.

Discussion Questions

1. Think about the process of sin James describes. What are some warning signs that the process has begun (that sin has been conceived)—signs that we can recognize before the process continues? How can we help each other with this?

2. Do we *have* to sin? Is it truly inevitable? Can we have victory over sin? How has all this played out in your life?

3. Why do you think James begins this passage by teaching that temptation doesn't come from God?

6

EVERY GOOD
AND PERFECT GIFT

Do not be deceived, my beloved brethren.
Every good thing given and every perfect gift is from above,
coming down from the Father of lights, with whom there is
no variation or shifting shadow. In the exercise of his will he
brought us forth by the word of truth, so that
we would be a kind of first fruits among his creatures.

JAMES 1:16-18

A s I write this, I'm on a diet, though it's not fashionable to call it that. I'm supposed to say it's a "lifestyle change" or "healthy eating," but it's a diet. I'm avoiding carbs and sugar, and I'm eating lots of protein, vegetables, and natural foods. My difficulty in adhering to the diet has revealed to me that I'm a glutton most of the time. And gluttony, the Bible tells us, is a sin.[16] We seldom think, talk, or write about gluttony, but that doesn't mean it isn't sinful. We can't allow social acceptance to define sin; sin is defined in God's word, and we have no power of veto.

On this diet, my weight has dropped, my blood pressure has improved, and I'm brighter, less bloated, and in a generally better frame of mind. But I still crave sugar and empty carbohydrates. If I lose my self-control and indulge those unhealthy addictions without restraint, which is a sin, I'll return to being less healthy. I can lie to myself by thinking such failure is inevitable, that I deserve to satisfy my appetite, and that my diet is preventing me from good things. But the consequence of undisciplined and unhealthy eating is poor health, a lower quality of life, and ultimately an earlier death, while the outcome of healthy eating is a healthier body and a richer life. By repenting of gluttony, I'm not missing out on a good thing, but avoiding a deadly thing.

So it is with all things in God's word—his commands do not prohibit good things, but point us to something better.

Having outlined sin's cycle of death, James now directs his brethren to the beautiful truth that our heavenly Father, the creator of all things, is also the giver of every good gift. This promise of good gifts is more than an alternative to the death wrought by sin; it's also a weapon against temptation toward sin.

One of the greatest obstacles to a joyful life in Christ is the false belief that sin has something better to offer. Eve succumbed to this lie in the garden just as we often succumb to the lie in our own lives. We believe greater joy will come from greed, drunkenness, or sexual licentiousness than from a righteous life of godly submission. In this, we're deceived. There's no good gift outside of what the Father intends for us. Satan's words to Eve in the garden implied that the Creator was holding back something good, something better than what she already had, though what she had was paradise undimmed. She was deceived, and consequently, death entered the world.

Note the comprehensive language James uses in 1:17: "*Every* good thing given and *every* perfect gift is from above." Therefore every enticing thing that's not from God is at best a cheap imitation of the better things God intends—or worse, a destructive idol intent on destroying our joy and our relationships. The bait dangles in front of us, promising what it can't deliver.

Money is a poor substitute for true security. Casual sex is a poor substitute for marital sexual intimacy. Alcohol is a poor substitute for joy. Drugs are a poor substitute for peace. Yet we accept these counterfeits and forfeit the good and perfect gifts. Why? Because we're deceived. We think God is withholding something good, when in fact he's protecting us from the bad and preparing us for the best.

Even the suffering that results from our sin has a purpose. Such suffering reveals the deception that there are good things outside of God. Such suffering drives us to seek the greater fulfillment God intends.

James starts this passage by saying, "Do not be deceived." Deceit comes in many forms. If the deceiver fails to convince us to reject God's best, he'll try to redefine what God's best is. This deceit has ensnared many Christians. In anticipation of this deceit, James points out that all good and perfect gifts come "from the Father of lights, with whom there is no variation of shifting of shadow." The phrase "Father of lights" was an ancient Jewish reference to God as creator.[17] "Lights" refers to the sun and stars in their perpetual courses. Tellingly, James chooses this description to emphasize God's unchanging nature. Times change, customs change, cultural mores change, and even God appears to change in the ways he deals with us. Yet from a broader perspective, God's nature and character are unchanging and unchangeable.

God's immutability is one of the most comforting things about him. "Jesus Christ is the same yesterday and today and forever" (Hebrews 13:8). He's not capricious or temperamental. God won't change the game or pull the rug out from under us. He's not a trickster. Yet we want a changing God when it comes to justifying our sinful behavior. Don't be deceived; in God there's no variation or shifting shadow.

There are those who would convince us—often in defense of sin—that God has evolved in what he considers good and what he considers evil. Some will point to obscure Levitical codes as an example of God's changing character. What the New Testament reflects is God's fulfillment of that law, not its abandonment. God gave the Levitical codes to point his people toward the coming Messiah. The Messiah came and fulfilled the purpose of the Jewish religious law. Christ himself said that he did not come to abolish the law, but to fulfill it (Matthew 5:17). The Father of lights hasn't changed, but since the coming of Christ, we're viewing those lights from another point on the timeline of history.

In their effort to claim that sinful behaviors are within the bounds of what God intends, many Christians either misunderstand or distort the concept of grace, confusing it with the redefinition of sin. In defense of sexual sin, many quote the words of Christ in John 8:7, during his encounter with the woman caught in adultery; in confronting the woman's hypocritical accusers, Jesus said, "Let him who is without sin cast the first stone." Many apologists for sexual sin neglect this story's ending, where Christ commands the adulterous woman to "Go. From now on sin no more" (John 8:11). In this story Christ evidenced true grace, which includes forgiveness, mercy, and restoration in the face of sin. Merely redefining sin is not grace at all. Ironically, this confusion of grace with a redefinition of sin has rendered many people incapable of true grace and unable to forgive what they choose to define or emphasize as sin. Those who tolerate sexual sin now hold the stones, and they don't hesitate to throw. They're deceived, and have deprived themselves of God's good and perfect gifts.

James concludes this passage by focusing on the best and most perfect gift given to any of us—our salvation. "In the exercise of his will he brought us forth by the word of truth." God intentionally exercised his will in bringing us to salvation. Our salvation didn't come about by accident or begrudging capitulation, but is the fruit of God's earnest desire to redeem his children. The phrase "bring forth" echoes the same phrasing in 1:15, where James says that sin brings forth (or gives birth to) death. God's gift of eternal life stands opposite the death brought about through sin. Salvation lifts the curse brought about by Adam and Eve in the garden. This gift is revealed now in part, and we still look forward to the day when "there will no longer be any death; there will no longer be any mourning, or crying or pain" (Revelation 21:4). This is our promise and our hope.

James describes us as a "kind of first fruits." Throughout Scripture, the concept of first fruits indicates God's portion, the things consecrated to him. We're his first fruits because he loves us and cherishes us. He desires to withhold no good thing from us (Psalm 84:11). Of course, this often seems not to be true. From where we stand on this earth, it's often hard to believe our God intends only good things for us, because circumstances are hard, and we suffer loss and pain. In difficult seasons, we must remember that the fulfillment of God's ambitions for us is still to be realized, and we must cultivate our hope for that coming day.[18]

To remember that God desires to give us good and perfect gifts is a powerful weapon against sin. If we believe that all good things come from God, and cultivate the hope that the best is still to come, we'll be less tempted toward lesser things. It's like the consistent consumption of healthy foods, which over time weakens our craving for unhealthy alternatives. When we diligently seek the greater things, we grow our appetite for the things of God, and the things of the world are no longer as appealing.

In the Old Testament, our unchanging God put a proposal to his people: "I have set before you life and death, the blessing and the curse. So choose life, in order that you may live" (Deuteronomy 30:19). The same choices are set before us today. What will we choose?

Don't be deceived; there's nothing good for us in this life outside of what God intends. What he intends for us is life abundant.

Discussion Questions

1. Think of a particular action, activity, or mindset that society currently calls good but the Bible describes as sin. How difficult is it for you to line up with the Bible's view as opposed to that of the world?
2. What kinds of lies accompany the thing that you identified in response to the first question? What truths does the Bible present to counter those lies?
3. How do you define grace? How do you think the Bible defines grace? What's an example of active grace that you've recently witnessed?

7

ON LISTENING
AND ANGER

This you know, my beloved brethren.
But everyone must be quick to hear,
slow to speak and slow to anger; for the anger of man
does not achieve the righteousness of God.
Therefore, putting aside all filthiness
and all that remains of wickedness,
in humility receive the word implanted,
which is able to save your souls.

JAMES 1:19-21

As I scrolled through the morning's Facebook feed, I saw birthday notifications, wedding pictures, and photos of nearly forgotten friends on glamorous vacations. Amid the benign news from friends and acquaintances, I also saw a particularly uninformed and offensive political post. My blood boiled. I felt that the post was directed at me in particular. I'd been down this path before, and I knew that silence was the best course, but I responded—at length, with vigor, and with an aggressive tone. I read and reread my post to ensure that I'd made no embarrassing grammatical errors that might blunt the impact of my elegant and persuasive essay.

For an hour after posting, I kept checking my feed to see who had "liked" or commented on my post. After refreshing my feed a few times, I saw that I'd received an equally aggressive and contrary reply. Other commenters weighed in, and soon people whose only connection in life was having me as a Facebook friend were exchanging harsh words. Over the course of the day, I interrupted my work, my peace, and my friendships while changing absolutely no one's mind. The fruit of my angry post was more anger, more division, and more obstacles to my walking in the righteousness of God.

James predates Facebook by two thousand years, but his wisdom concerning speaking and anger has never been more applicable than today.

James 1:19 begins with, "This you know," which could also be interpreted as "Know this,"[19] an urgent exhortation for his readers to know and do the things he discusses. He describes these readers as "beloved brethren," indicating that he's talking not to unbelievers but to believers in Jesus Christ who are struggling to live this way.

James then tells us that we're to "be quick to hear." That seems an odd command, because to be quick implies movement, but we think of hearing as passive. This suggests that we need to improve our understanding of hearing. A good listener is an active listener, engaged in what's being said, and not merely providing silence into which someone can speak. When I'm reading a book and my wife is talking to me, I'm quiet, but I'm not listening (something my wife has learned over the years). When I'm truly listening—truly hearing her—I'm looking at her, reflecting back what she has said, and repeating and rephrasing so I can be sure

I understand. I ask questions to show I'm interested in what she has to say and I want to know more.

As a society, our listening skills are diminishing. In our effort to be heard, we rarely hear others. Note that James is talking to people who are enduring the trial of persecution. His instruction to be "quick to hear" applies therefore to people who are in a hostile environment. The context implies that he's instructing these people to be quick to hear even their persecutors. We're exposed to things that offend us every day. What does it mean to be "quick to hear" in this environment? It certainly doesn't mean to agree with all that's being said. But we must still hear the people around us, listening to even the offending voices, because they come from people we're called to lead into the kingdom of God.

Paul writes, "If I speak with the tongues of men and of angels, but do not have love, I have become a noisy gong or a clanging cymbal" (1 Corinthians 13:1). If we speak without love—which is often speaking without listening—no one will hear us. All they can hear is the brassy, offensive noise coming out of the mouth of someone who hasn't even taken the time to hear. No matter how correct our positions might be, no one will hear us if our words aren't uttered in love. Yet in our desire to be heard, we're slow to listen, we're quick to speak, and we manage to offend without effectively communicating the truth.

Much of our interaction today is on social media. Most of us have a diverse group of people in our social media networks, so we often read other people's disagreeable opinions. It's tempting to react, but a reaction through social media is rarely helpful. I'm saddened by the shrill tenor of communications on social media or on news site commentary, not so much from the enemies of faith, which is to be expected, but from people who purport to follow Jesus. The tone is often condescending, self-righteous, and shrill, sometimes including gleeful predictions of eternal damnation for those who oppose the faith.

What if instead—not just on social media but in all our interaction—we could acknowledge the deeper needs (such as loneliness, confusion, doubt, and fear) being expressed by people holding opinions contrary to ours. But instead of being quick to listen, we're quick to speak. Sometimes we don't let the speaker finish at all. Even while someone else is speaking, we're formulating our reply, and we end up responding to something anticipated rather than something said.

This concept isn't just for dealing with perceived enemies, but also (perhaps especially) with our spouse, children, siblings, and parents. In order to be heard, we must first listen. There's an inherent sacrifice in listening, a laying down of our own interests to give someone else the floor. This setting aside of our own interest is the life to which we're called as Christians. The world is supposed to know we're Christians by our love for one another, but disputes within our families and our communities of faith can often be more vicious than those outside.

James links our speech and our anger. We're to be both slow to speak and slow to become angry. The speed with which we become angry is a fair barometer of our spiritual health. With the proper anger triggers, how long does it take you to go from zero to ten on the anger scale? Our anger often produces quick, rash, and imprudent speech. We convince ourselves that we're right, and feel justified in responding angrily with harsh words. But James tells us that the anger of man doesn't achieve the righteousness of God.

Our anger often wounds, demeans, and produces anger in others. Our anger makes others feel small, weak, and insignificant. Our anger quenches our spouse's affection and stimulates our children's rebelliousness. Anger produces a maelstrom of sin and fractured relationships.

Is it really a sin to be angry? After all, didn't Jesus get angry? Isn't righteous indignation not only justified but sometimes necessary? Consider those questions in light of these verses in Proverbs:

A man's discretion makes him slow to anger, and it is his glory to overlook a transgression. (19:11)

There is one who speaks rashly like the thrusts of a sword, but the tongue of the wise brings healing. (12:18)

He who is slow to anger has great understanding, but he who is quick-tempered exalts folly. (14:29)

A fool gives full vent to his anger; but a wise man keeps himself under control. (29:11)

Scripture consistently warns of the danger of anger. It's not always a sin to be angry; Jesus himself got angry. There's such a thing as righteous indignation. However, in identifying an exception to a rule, we must not forget the rule.

The most notable example of Jesus's anger was when he threw over the money-changers' tables in the temple because he was consumed with zeal for his Father's house (Matthew 21:12-13). Three key factors distinguish Jesus's anger from our typical anger. First, Jesus was God. We don't have the same license that a perfect God does to inflict righteous zeal on sinners. Second, Jesus was consumed with zeal for this Father's house, not for his own personal interests. Let's be brutally honest with ourselves—is our anger really stemming from zeal for God, or from personal offense? Our anger often comes from threatened loss of control, from disrespect, or when someone else's error causes us personal expense or inconvenience. Third, our anger is often fueled by fear, and fear wasn't present in Jesus's cleansing wrath. Unlike Jesus's righteous anger, our anger doesn't lead to the righteousness of God.

James gives us the alternative to anger, "Therefore, putting aside all filthiness and all the remains of wickedness, in humility receive the word implanted, which is able to save your souls." In lieu of speaking, we're to listen, and in lieu of being angry, in humility we're to allow the word of God to dwell in us. Unlike our anger, the word of God does produce righteousness and salvation.

In the midst of this noisy and angry world, we easily succumb to the lie that our own anger is an effective weapon. Rather than noisy anger, Christ has modeled for us quiet endurance in the face of insult (1 Peter 2:23). There's a measure of suffering in this. Through our own quiet endurance, we participate in the fellowship of his sufferings and the power of his resurrection (Philippians 3:10). In enduring insult, we become more like him, which is what it means to become a for-real Christian.

Discussion Questions

1. Why is it so hard to listen?
2. How can you tell when someone's not listening to you? What does this teach you about effective listening?
3. What prompts you to anger? If your anger isn't righteous anger, how might you better respond to these prompts?

8

TO BE
IS TO DO

Therefore, putting aside all filthiness and all that remains of
wickedness, in humility receive the word implanted, which is
able to save your souls. But prove yourselves doers of the word
and not merely hearers who delude themselves. For if anyone is
a hearer of the word and not a doer, he is like a man who looks
at his natural face in a mirror; for once he has looked at himself
and gone away, he has immediately forgotten what kind of person he was. But one who looks intently at the perfect law, the law
of liberty, and abides by it, not having become a forgetful hearer
but an effectual doer, this man will be blessed in what he does.

JAMES 1:21-25

I sat with my mentor at a popular breakfast spot in Atlanta,
arguing with him, yet desperately wanting to believe what he
had to say. Sometimes we push back against encouragement
because we need our encouragers to push back harder still. I was
struggling with an inescapable sense of failure, despite the fact
I'd recently landed my dream job. I had a beautiful wife and two
young children, and my professional life had taken a demonstrable

turn for the better, but I felt like I was only one misstep away from losing it all. Everything seemed to balance precariously on my imperfect shoulders, and the weight was crushing me. I sought the answer in the form of improved performance through greater effort, but my mentor was telling me to rest.

My mentor preached, "Your old life has been buried with Jesus in his death, and just as he was raised from death, you have been raised to newness of life! Everything in your life that counts is what he has accomplished in you. There's no performing, there's no earning, there's no deserving. He's the provider and protector for your family. Rest in him and abide in him." My mentor preached the same message whenever we met, because it was the message I needed to hear.

It all sounded wonderful, and none of it was altogether new to me. In fact, I could quote from memory most of the scriptures he was using. My mentor's words carried weight because his life evidenced real belief. Still, I wrestled. As wonderful as it all sounded, there was a gap between my hearing and my believing.

I pushed back, "But with all this resting and abiding, there's got to be some doing, right? I mean, simply having this conversation isn't going to change everything. Isn't there anything I can do?"

"Yes," he answered. "There is something you can do."

Christians rightly believe that Jesus has accomplished the necessary things in connection with our salvation, and we rest in this accomplished work. We don't work to earn God's favor, which is a gift of grace. But the journey to Christian maturity is not passive. James 1:21-25 addresses the "doing" that plays a role in our becoming for-real Christians.

First, James encourages us to set aside all filthiness and all that remains of wickedness. Many of us persist in conduct we know is sinful and destructive, and still manage to be frustrated when God doesn't give us greater peace. We need to lay aside our old patterns of conduct, speech, and thinking. Only then can we move forward in our spiritual walk—unencumbered, clean, and in the likeness of God.

Second, we must humbly receive the word implanted in us. Like a farmer sowing seed, God has sown his word on our hearts (Matthew 13:1-23). His word is revealed in Scripture. Rather than receiving this word, we often neglect or fight it. We fill our minds and hearts with all manner of distractions and entertainment, but we neglect the eternal word of truth revealed in Scripture. When we do come to the word of God, we come seeking to justify preexisting beliefs and behavior rather than seeking to be changed. If we cease neglecting and stop resisting, God's word brings salvation—which is not only the saving of our souls, but also deliverance into all the good promises of God.

Third, we must do what the word says. When we hear but do not do, we deceive ourselves. We deceive ourselves into thinking that we're fruitful, that we're growing in our faith, and that we're living the life to which God has called us. We're deceived if we think that attending church, reading Christian books, and singing praise music are sufficient to grow us up in Christ. It's insufficient to listen; we must change, and we must be doers.

Fourth, we must remember who we are in light of God's word. We're his children. He therefore loves us, has forgiven us, and has wonderful things in store for us. A great deal of the Christian walk is the simple discipline of remembering these things. When we forget, we lose our peace and our direction. When we forget, our emotions ride the great swings of circumstance. When we forget, we easily succumb to despair and discouragement. James gives us the antidote to forgetfulness: looking intently at the perfect law, the law of liberty.

When the word "perfect" appears in Scripture, think "complete." Christ said that he came not to abolish the law, but to fulfill it—he completed it. That's why we no longer have to follow the ceremonial law of the Old Testament. Those rituals pointed Jews toward the Messiah who was to come, and now he has come. The moral law of God remains after Christ, but even that moral law isn't the perfect law. The moral law is perfect only insofar as it has been satisfied, and it has been satisfied, or perfected, only in Christ. The perfect law is God's law as fulfilled in Christ.

But what does James mean in 1:25 by describing the perfect law as "the law of liberty"? Paul writes, "Now the Lord is the Spirit, and where the Spirit of the Lord is, there is liberty" (2 Corinthians 3:17). In Romans 8, Paul writes, "The law of the Spirit of life in Christ Jesus has set you free from the law of sin and of death. For what the law could not do, weak as it was through the flesh, God did: sending his own Son in the likeness of sinful flesh and as an offering for sin" (Romans 8:2). The law of liberty doesn't mean we're free to do whatever we want without consequence. The law of liberty means that because the Spirit of God is in us, we're free from the law of sin and death—we don't have to keep doing the things that lead to death. We're no longer slaves to sin, but servants of God.

The person who's a hearer and not a doer is like a man who glances at his identity as a free and redeemed man in light of the law of liberty, but turns away and immediately forgets what kind of person he is. He forgets how he's supposed to act, think, and speak—and respond to trials—because he has forgotten what kind of person he is.

When we look intently at the perfect law, the law of liberty, and don't look away, we remember who we are and whose we are. This brings changes in how we think, feel, and behave, and we bear good fruit.

For many Christians, the Bible's promise of an abundant life carries the taint of broken promise rather than joyful hope. You might ask, "Why don't I experience that abundance? I've been a believer in Jesus Christ for many years, and I still feel like I carry life's weight on my shoulders. I don't feel free at all. I feel shackled to my own inadequacy and enslaved to the whims of circumstance." I sympathize, because I also struggle with these thoughts. To fight against them, we can look together at James's statement that we must be doers and not merely hearers of God's word.

There's a wonderful promise for the person who's an effectual doer rather than a forgetful hearer: he'll be blessed in what he does. Step away from your burdens by looking intently at the perfect law of God, the law of liberty, and remember who you are in light of Christ's accomplished work.

Discussion Questions

1. What are some examples of impurity that Christians frequently tolerate? What would repentance from these things look like?

2. What are the practical ways in which we can "receive the word of God"? Describe a time in your life when God's word was particularly effective in changing you or someone you know.

3. Name and describe someone in your personal experience who was an effective doer of God's word. Does that sort of life seem unattainable to you? Do you desire to imitate it?

9

DO YOU THINK
YOURSELF RELIGIOUS?

If anyone thinks himself to be religious,
and yet does not bridle his tongue but deceives
his own heart, this man's religion is worthless.
Pure and undefiled religion
in the sight of our God and Father is this:
to visit orphans and widows in their distress,
and to keep oneself unstained by the world.

JAMES 1:26-27

I stared at the blinking cursor on my computer screen. A friend had messaged me to say that what matters about our Christianity is what we do for others here and now, not what we believe about the hereafter. Heaven was too abstract to motivate her, and she felt that conventional Christianity was too narrow to provide hope for a hurting world. She was prompted to write this after a debate with a mutual friend, another Christian, who emphasized upright moral conduct and conservative political positions. He spoke of the unsaved peoples of the world as if they were a contaminant to be avoided rather than people to be loved.

Both sides of this debate were missing some essentials, and neither was dealing with the other in grace. As my cursor flashed, I considered my response. Looking back, I'd have done well to direct her to James 1:26-27.

Many people who call themselves Christian fall into one of two camps. One group emphasizes a social justice ethic that ministers to the poor and oppressed peoples of the earth. The other group emphasizes moral uprightness, with an emphasis on sexual purity, avoidance of substance abuse, and proper language. Both groups think they've got a handle on what's most important about being a Christian. But what makes us Christian is neither adhering to an ethic of service nor moral excellence in other areas. What makes us Christians is our belief in Jesus Christ, the Son of God, crucified and raised from the dead (John 3:15; Acts 16:31; Romans 3:22; Ephesians 1:13).

What James addresses in 1:26-27 is not what makes us Christians, but how Christians should behave. James is describing the outward appearance of a truly religious person. When it comes to the divide between those emphasizing a social ethic and those focusing on moral purity, James doesn't allow for an either/or; he calls us to both/and.

James's use of the word "religious" in 1:26 refers to a devout, diligent performer of outward service to God,[20] although such outward service isn't necessarily superficial. It's simply the observable religious behavior of someone who professes belief in God. We often think of our faith as an invisible thing that happens inside us. But James's letter tells us that the outside things also count. In fact, the surest indicator of a true inner faith is its outward manifestation.

James begins his discussion of true religion by talking about the importance of the tongue. If a person thinks himself religious but spews irreligious things from his mouth, then he's deceived. The man who cannot bridle his tongue is far from God. Jesus himself described this connection between heart and tongue:

> A good man brings good things out of the good stored up in his heart, and an evil man brings evil things out of the evil stored up in his heart. For the mouth speaks what the heart is full of. (Luke 6:45)

What comes out of your mouth? Is it gossip, angry words, complaining, envy, bitterness? If so, James says, then your religion—the outward manifestation of your inner belief—is worthless. We can pretend to be something other than we are, but our tongues eventually reveal our true selves. We may think of ourselves as having a compassionate social ethic, or as being holy and righteous, but we're greatly mistaken about that if our speech is laced with vitriol and contempt for other people.

I've described what should be absent in our speech, but what should be present? What should speech reveal as being present in the heart of the for-real Christian? James tells us that our speech should reflect both a compassion for the oppressed and a holy devotion to God.

True and undefiled religion in the eyes of God our Father (the only eyes that count) is to visit orphans and widows in their distress. James refers here not to financial provision, but to visitation. Other scriptures call us to meet financial needs, but James here focuses on something else. To "visit" means to regard or look at someone closely, and especially with mercy.[21] When Jesus healed, he usually touched the afflicted. He regarded them and attended to them personally, especially those whom the rest of the world considered untouchable.

Governments of the western world generally buffer orphans and widows from homelessness or starvation, so unless we travel to impoverished parts of the world, we're rarely confronted with the immediate physical needs of the widow or orphan. Consequently, some Christians consider their social obligations fulfilled with the payment of taxes. A somewhat more sensitive person will give money above and beyond the legal requirement. But the person with a true and undefiled religion will interact with widows and orphans, looking upon them with regard, with intention, and with mercy.

Though our government-created social safety nets serve a limited purpose, they've also contributed to a disconnect between the church and the poor. Where the word "charity" was once synonymous with love, it's now synonymous with the distant, sanitized writing of a check. To give of our time is often harder, more consuming, and ultimately far more rewarding than sending our dollars. This is why God calls us to look upon the poor. Our attentive regard will minister to the oppressed in ways that cash alone cannot. In true Christian service, we bring Jesus, and not just our money, to those in distress. Jesus had the power to grant wealth to every person he encountered, but he didn't. He called his disciples to minister to the poor instead. Ministering to those in distress changes both the served and the servant.

Christian charity is not the whole of "true religion." James tells us that in the eyes of God our Father, true and undefiled religion is keeping ourselves unstained by the world. Instead of aiming for purity, many of us push the boundaries of our liberty in Christ, often ignoring the following warning from the apostle Paul.

> What then? Shall we sin because we are not under the law but under grace? By no means! Don't you know that when you offer yourselves to someone as obedient slaves, you are slaves of the one you obey—whether you are slaves to sin, which leads to death, or to obedience, which leads to righteousness? (Romans 6:15-16)

The lives of too many Christians are indistinguishable from the rest of the world with respect to sexual licentiousness, abuse of alcohol, greed, and integrity. We don't earn our salvation by abstaining from sin, and we don't lose salvation by sinning. But we do choose slavery to the hollow, idolatrous systems of this world when we choose to sin rather than pursue holiness. We're often more concerned with being acceptable to the world than pleasing to God. We choose to be cool rather than to be holy. We deceive ourselves in thinking that such behavior endears us to the world and enhances our ministry, when in fact lost people yearn to encounter Christians who combine compassion with moral integrity. When our lives are full of sin, we advance the notion that Christ is little more than the long-dead preacher of a noble ethic rather than the living and sovereign Creator of the universe—and our final judge.

The for-real Christian cannot choose between serving the oppressed and striving for holiness, because the abiding presence of Christ within the Christian produces a person who desires to serve the needy while also living a holy life. There's no Christian service and no Christian goodness outside of Christ.

We complain that we don't feel loved by God or close to him, that we lack the joy and passion we once had for him. We try to recapture intimacy through emotional worship services—but the passion dies as the music fades. Worship services are wonderful and necessary, but they're not enough. If the sum total of our religious experience is a passionate worship service, then we aren't engaged in the true religion to which James calls us. We experience intimacy with God when we're engaged in his work. Stop resisting the very thing that will produce the lost intimacy you crave.

If all who call themselves Christian would guard their tongue, visit widows and orphans in distress, and keep themselves unstained by the world, how different this world would be! One survey found that 77 percent of the U.S. population considers itself Christian,[22] but the prevalence of violence and fear and persistent social ills suggests that many among those 77 percent are deceived and subscribing to a worthless religion. James calls us to a religion that's both inward and outward. He calls us to a world-changing faith that necessarily draws on the power of the living Christ.

Live the both/and of serving the least and living the holy life to which God has called you. You'll lose only what needs to be lost, and you'll gain an eternal inheritance worthy of your hope.

Discussion Questions

1. Most of us fall on one side or other of the divide between those who emphasize a Christian social ethic and those who emphasize moral and doctrinal purity. Where do you find yourself?

2. How has today's political landscape affected the unity of the church and public perceptions of the Christian faith? What

is the Christian's role with respect to politics in a democratic society?

3. On whichever side of the divide you find yourself, what might be an effective step to adopt a both/and mentality in the working out of your faith?

10

SEEING BEYOND
THE SUPERFICIAL

My brethren, do not hold your faith in our glorious
Lord Jesus Christ with an attitude of personal favoritism.
For if a man comes into your assembly with a gold ring and
dressed in fine clothes, and there also comes in a poor man in
dirty clothes, and you pay special attention to the one who is
wearing the fine clothes, and say, "You sit here in a good place,"
and you say to the poor man, "You stand over there, or sit down
by my footstool," have you not made distinctions among
yourselves, and become judges with evil motives?

JAMES 2:1-4

ost of us walk through life feeling as if we're on the outside looking in. For much of my life, I've felt as though I
was insufficiently attractive, athletic, successful, or witty
to be fully accepted. I've carried with me a vague sense of inferiority, of rejection, and of exclusion.

In sharing this feeling with others, I've learned that this
self-perception is surprisingly common. If you were to take a poll
of any given group of people—at school, the office, your church,

or your neighborhood—you'd likely find that a majority of people feel like outsiders. Why is this feeling so common? One reason is that we reflexively judge other people based on superficial characteristics while assuming that everyone else does the same. We're terrified that other people are doing what we do, which is to assess someone's value based on what we can immediately see.

James's command against personal favoritism is among his most challenging because it's one of the most countercultural. For most of us, making superficial assessments of people comes as naturally as breathing—we enter a room and immediately size up the crowd, determine where we rank, and identify the people with whom we should connect. These days, if there's a famous person in the room we might even try to get close enough to include them in a selfie. This is noxious enough outside the church, but we often bring this same attitude into the church and evaluate the people who come into our fellowship based on outward appearance. We carry false assumptions that the more prosperous looking people are also more godly, more worthy of respect, and more suited to leadership. James calls us to see beyond these superficial things.

The word "faith" is a reference to the entirety of our belief system, not just the act of believing for salvation.[23] Therefore when James tells us in 2:1, "Do not hold your faith…with an attitude of personal favoritism," he's warning us against having a belief system that distinguishes among people based on their earthly status. James demonstrates the absurdity of this sort of personal favoritism when he describes the object of our faith as being "our glorious Lord Jesus Christ." Christians are people once defined by sin but now defined by Christ. When we deal with each other in an attitude of personal favoritism, we demean the glorious work of Christ by focusing on superficial and meaningless earthly distinctions.

Jesus's human origins and ministry were notably humble. Christ's ancestors included Tamar, who posed as a prostitute in order to seduce her father-in-law; Rahab, a Gentile prostitute; Ruth, a Gentile idol-worshiper; Bathsheba, the adulterer; and Jeconiah, a disgraced and cursed king. If the author of history had wanted to create a more prestigious earthly lineage for the Messiah, he could have. Instead, he chose to include the humble and the fallen in Christ's genealogy. Jesus was born in a stable among beasts. He chose humble men as his disciples, and he lived a nomadic life without a permanent place to lay his head. He died the death of a common criminal. No part of Jesus's life was oriented toward earthly status, and his words to the rich and powerful were usually critical, challenging the power structures of the day.

In James's day, gold rings were a mark of wealth and high social standing. Historical sources suggest that merchants in Jerusalem made money by renting out gold rings to people who wanted to look prosperous. They sometimes wore a ring on every finger as a status symbol.[24] Today, such a display would be curious, but not status-enhancing.

What are the markers of status—the "gold rings"—we look for today? Consider the questions we ask (either to others or ourselves) when we meet someone for the first time.

Where do you live? Many of us assign prestige to certain neighborhoods or school districts. Asking people where they live helps us to organize them in our mental file cabinet. We hold certain cities or states of origin to be more prestigious than others. Based on where others live, we draw conclusions about their financial status, their education, and their importance in our community. Jesus grew up in the humble town of Nazareth in the region of Galilee, an area held in contempt by the upper crust of

Jerusalem society. Other than fulfillment of prophecy, Christ had no interest in geographic origins.

Where did you go to school? Here in the South, we're likely thinking more about football than education when we ask that question, but we nevertheless categorize people based on their answer. I went to a small Christian college few people have heard of, and I often have to explain where it's located and why I chose to attend there. When we ask where someone went to school, we're not usually being snobbish or cruel. In fact, we're often just trying to make conversation. But reflect on what your mind does with that information. Some part of your brain ranks people based on where they went to school. We draw conclusions about whether someone is smart, connected, or hard-working. We answer our own internal questions: Is this someone I would like to know more, someone I can talk to, someone I'd like to spend more time with?

But what kind of value did Jesus attach to education? If he highly valued education, he would have chosen religious leaders from the synagogues who'd served under noted rabbis. Instead, most of his disciples were humble and uneducated laborers. After Pentecost, Peter and John were interrogated by a group of religious leaders and highly educated men of high priestly descent. The Spirit provided Peter and John with the right words to speak in this stressful situation, just as Jesus promised (Luke 12:11-12). Luke tells us that as these leaders and priests "observed the confidence of Peter and John and understood that they were uneducated and untrained men, they were amazed and began to recognize them as having been with Jesus" (Acts 4:13). Jesus chose ordinary, unschooled men so that no one would mistake the power they held for the earthly power that comes from high education. People would instead observe, "They've been with Jesus."

If you're a parent, which situation would you rather have for your children: their impressing others just by mentioning the prestigious school they attended, or their causing people to conclude, "They've been with Jesus"?

Consider further the kinds of evaluations we quickly make when we meet someone for the first time:

Is she pretty? Our culture is obsessed with beauty. Our economic system would collapse if beauty ceased to be a virtue, because every year we devote billions of dollars to appearing youthful, with clear skin, thin bodies, and luxurious hair. We're drawn to beautiful people, and we attribute to them all sorts of positive traits unconnected with physical beauty. We envy beauty, covet it, and often make it an idol. Yet, what does Scripture say about physical appearance?

In the Old Testament, Samuel the judge went to Jesse's house to anoint the next king of Israel, not yet knowing who that would be. Jesse paraded his sons before Samuel one by one. When Samuel saw Jesse's oldest—tall, imposing, and handsome—he thought that surely the Lord's anointed stood before him. But God responded, "Do not look at his appearance or at the height of his stature, because I have rejected him; for God sees not as a man sees, for man looks at outward appearance, but the Lord looks at the heart" (1 Samuel 16:7).

In Proverbs 31:10 we're told, "Charm is deceptive and beauty is fleeting, but a woman who fears the Lord, she shall be praised" (Proverbs 31:10). Many of our women carry a sense of inferiority because they don't measure up to the air-brushed and artificially enhanced models on the covers of magazines. We men add to this insecurity by bowing at the same altar. In this we're all failing to appreciate what the Lord appreciates, which is the content of the heart.

Is he athletic? This is a measuring stick for men in particular. In our youth, we highly esteem the classmate who's a talented athlete for our high school team. In later life, we grant respect to a man simply because he has a low handicap in golf. Men who play collegiate or professional sports sometimes earn the equivalent of an annuity, with speaking gigs and appearance fees based largely on what they were able to accomplish on the athletic field. We devote many hours of our week to watching the exploits of men who've won the genetic lottery and ply their trade in a stadium. Yet Paul writes, "Bodily discipline is only of little profit, but godliness is profitable for all things, since it holds promise for the present life and also for the life to come" (1 Timothy 4:8).

How is she dressed? I confess to being tone deaf on this one. I don't place much stock in what someone's wearing because I have no idea what's fashionable. I leave all style decisions to my wife or my kids. However, style is another marker of status for many. I've encountered some people who view style as higher virtue than integrity or kindness.

Noted designers create a style or label distinctive enough to be recognized. We buy handbags, shoes, or garments not for their utility, but because of the status they project. Why do we do this? Because people think differently about us when we wear those clothes; they conclude that we're both successful and in the know.

When I was in elementary school, I desperately wanted an Izod Lacoste shirt for Christmas (the golf shirt with the alligator logo). I was terrified that my wonderfully frugal mother would buy the discount store version emblazoned with a different logo, but my self-esteem required an alligator. They may have been exactly the same shirt, but the logo made all the difference. I'm sure that when I wore my Izod shirt on the first day back at school, the cool kids barely noticed, and the poorer kids felt a little worse about themselves, but in the moment I felt pretty good. What does Scripture say about clothes? In Christ's telling of the story of the rich man and Lazarus, the rich man (who went to hell) was described as being "habitually dressed in purple and fine linen, joyously living in splendor every day" (Luke 16:19). Yet it was the poor man in poor cloth who went to Abraham's bosom.

"What do you do for a living?" This is one of the most loaded questions we ask, and we ask it all the time. We don't generally ask it out of any ill will, yet it's freighted with baggage. How many of us are guilty of drawing a dozen conclusions about a person because of his answer to this question? How much deference, leadership opportunity, and respect do we give someone who works in the "right" profession or holds a sufficiently senior title, when in fact we should be looking to the deeper things that God esteems?

Is it wrong to live in a nice neighborhood, to attend a prestigious school, to succeed in sports, to dress well, to be beautiful, or to have a highly esteemed career? No, of course not. These things can be wonderful gifts from God that we can employ to his glory. But when we treat people differently based on how they measure up to these superficial criteria, we're guilty of failing to see people as God does, because God values the inner character of the heart.

All these superficial judgments are at play within the church, and we add others as well. Some believers judge each other according to a set of spiritual-seeming yet external factors. What does she let her kids watch on TV? Does she let them have access to electronic devices? Where do her kids go to school? How many small groups is that person in? Can he flip to a Bible passage without looking at the table of contents? Does he wear a tie to church? Does he golf on Sunday? While these all may relate to wise and well-considered decisions we make for ourselves and for our families, we shouldn't draw conclusions about a person's spiritual health based on these superficial things. The danger of focusing on these external things is that we become far more concerned with mere appearances. This leads to tremendous spiritual dysfunction.

James says that when we succumb to personal favoritism, we make distinctions among ourselves and we become judges with evil motives. In this context, judging means evaluating a person's worth based on external things without significance in the kingdom of God. The "evil motives" James speaks of have to do with our selfishly wanting to align ourselves with people who enhance our status. In this, we're serving our own interests rather than loving one another, and Jesus tells us that our love for each other is how the world will know we're Christians.

It's difficult to stop personal favoritism because partiality comes so naturally to us, but think of the freedom available to us if we could shed it! If we truly didn't care about markers of status and stopped comparing ourselves to other people, consider how much better we could love other people and be at peace with ourselves. What would our lives look like if we allowed God to free us from our slavery to image maintenance? In place of these false things, God will fill us with the true and enduring things of the kingdom—the wondrous fruits of the Spirit that flourish when we shed the things of this earth and see as God sees.

Discussion Questions

1. Most of us have particular areas in which we instinctively categorize people. In what area do you do this? Once you've categorized a person in this way, how does it affect your relationship with them?

2. Have you ever felt categorized by someone in a way you thought was unfair or offensive?

3. Because judging by external appearances is so automatic, how can we realistically change our judgmental heart?

11

WOULD YOU RATHER BE POOR OR RICH?

Listen, my beloved brethren: did not God choose
the poor of this world to be rich in faith and heirs
of the kingdom which he promised to those who love him?
But you have dishonored the poor man. Is it not the rich
who oppress you and personally drag you into court?
Do they not blaspheme
the fair name by which you have been called?

JAMES 2:5-7

In October of 2008, my wife and I, along with some friends, rented a mountain house for the weekend. Set in the shadow of Grandfather Mountain in western North Carolina, the house was massive to the point of excess, a monument to the gilded age of the immediately preceding years. But the economy had been teetering for months as we encountered headlines about a declining stock market, a government takeover of Fannie Mae and Freddie Mac, and the failures of Bear Stearns and Lehman Brothers. On the Friday we arrived at the "cabin," the

Dow Jones Index hit an unthinkable low of 7,882, reflecting a loss in value of more than 43 percent from its July 2007 high. We ate, drank, laughed, and enjoyed each other's company, but the specter of the crisis loomed large. There was a sense of finality in our celebration, a sober realization that a season of prosperity was ending. For me, the coming season of financial and professional uncertainty would be simultaneously the most terrifying and glorious of my life.

I work in commercial real estate, which was particularly hard hit in the crisis. Throughout my career to that point, I'd had more work than I wanted, never failing to bill the required number of hours or collect the expected fees at my firm. At the end of 2008, my clients went quiet, and some dissolved altogether. The entire industry was in a daze, and for the first time in my life, I had little to do at the office.

One day I went for a walk in Ansley Park, a residential area near my office in Atlanta's midtown financial district. Such a thing was unthinkable in busier days. There were a number of business people strolling along the sidewalks just like me; it was an odd scene. A resident standing in her front yard asked me, "What's going on? Why are all these people walking around?" I told her, "I think we're all just trying to figure out what to do."

Before the crisis of 2008, I talked a good game about trusting in God, but my trust wasn't in God. I was trusting in my skill, my degrees, a healthy economy, and money in the bank. When the financial crisis threatened my ability to provide for my family, I despaired. God revealed to me that I'd been trusting in an idol rather than in him. He provided lavishly for me in that season, in ways that defy explanation; I would be dishonoring him to say otherwise. But his greatest gift through that time was forcing me into a position of joyful dependence.

For much of the crisis, I thought money would be the solution to my problems. I planned to learn a new skill set, attract a new client, or figure out how to benefit from the crisis. I kept hitting walls. It was as if God was saying, "No, I won't let you find deliverance somewhere else. You'll learn that I am good, and that I am enough."

Do you want to be rich? If you've spent enough time in church, you probably know that the correct answer is no. But let's get to the heart of the matter. How would you complete this phrase: "If only I had _____, I could be at peace; I could stop worrying, and everything would be okay." How you fill in that blank reveals where you're placing your hope. If you fill the blank with anything other than "more of Jesus," you're looking to idols to make you whole.

The Bible is full of warnings against the love of money. This is because we often seek money instead of God for our provision, protection, and hope. Money is history's most persistent idol. Consider the following passages regarding wealth:

> Do not weary yourself to gain wealth, cease from your consideration of it. When you set your eyes on it, it is gone. For wealth certainly makes itself wings like an eagle that flies toward the heavens. (Proverbs 23:45)

> But woe to you who are rich, for you are receiving your comfort in full. (Luke 6:24)

> Do not store up for yourselves treasures on earth. (Matthew 6:19)

He who trusts in his riches will fall, but the righteous will flourish like the green leaf. (Proverbs 11:28)

Beware, and be on your guard against every form of greed; for not even when one has an abundance does his life consist of his possessions. (Luke 12:15)

Make sure that your character is free from the love of money, being content with what you have; for he himself has said, "I will never desert you, nor will I ever forsake you," so that we confidently say, "The Lord is my helper, I will not be afraid. What will man do to me?" (Hebrews 13:5)

It is easier for a camel to go through the eye of a needle than for a rich man to enter the kingdom of God. (Mark 10:25)

Do you still want to be rich? You might answer, "No, I don't want to be rich, but I'd like to have enough money so I never have to worry." If you'd like to at least be wealthy enough that you don't have to depend on God, then yes, you want to be rich.

In light of Scripture's warning against love of wealth, why do we Christians still desire to be rich? Let's be honest, most of us still do. I'm not immune. We say we believe the Bible, and we claim to rejoice in our dependence on God, yet most of us aspire to obtain wealth. There's an entire "Christian" industry devoted to helping Christians get rich and convincing them that the accumulation of riches is both a godly aspiration and evidence of God's favor—all in direct opposition to God's words quoted above. Such thinking keeps Christians in perpetual infancy.

There are two primary reasons we Christians want to be

rich, and they're related. First, we don't really believe in God, at least not enough to actually trust him. Jesus is a hedge, a socially acceptable add-on to an otherwise ordinary life. Sure, in the elementary cosmology of good versus evil, we side with the good. We agree that the Bible offers useful wisdom and that Jesus preached a noble ethic, and we enjoy the emotional catharsis of worship. But in every practical area of our lives, we live in a manner indistinguishable from everyone around us. We're functional atheists.

It's very uncomfortable to trust, at an essential level, in a God we cannot see. Therefore we pursue the security the world offers while professing to trust in God. However, as Christ teaches in his Sermon on the Mount, we cannot hold to those two things simultaneously. "No one can serve two masters; for either he will hate the one and love the other, or he will be devoted to one and despise the other. You cannot serve God and wealth" (Matthew 6:24). In our effort to take hold of both, we obtain neither. If a man places his hope in riches, he can never have enough material wealth to feel truly and permanently secure. Insofar as any of us have placed our hope in worldly wealth, we'll fail to know the peace of total dependence on God.

The second reason we want to be rich is fear. We have real and pressing needs, and we cannot see how God will meet them. Maybe we've already lost a house or suffered a serious financial setback, and we ask ourselves, "Where was God then?" Perhaps we fear that God's level of provision will be lower than we want it to be. In this, as in so many things, worship is critical to spiritual health. That may seem like a non sequitur, but it's in worship that we turn our attention to our Creator and celebrate his attributes. When we're worshiping well, we focus our attentions on our heavenly Father, and our earthly cares dim by comparison. In worship, we begin to recognize that what we really need is more of Jesus. As we worship, we can take confidence in Christ's words concerning our earthly necessities: "Your heavenly Father knows that you need all these things. But seek first his kingdom and his righteousness, and all these things will be added to you" (Matthew 6:31-34).

Consider the following verses extolling God's provision:

The thief comes only to steal and kill and destroy; I came that they may have life, and have it abundantly. (John 10:10)

And my God will supply all your needs according to his riches in glory in Christ Jesus. (Philippians 4:19)

I know how to get along with humble means, and I also know how to live in prosperity; in any and every circumstance I have learned the secret of being filled and going hungry, both of having abundance and suffering need. (Philippians 4:12)

He who trusts the Lord will prosper. (Proverbs 28:25)

The Lord will not allow the righteous to hunger. (Proverbs 10:3)

In the Sermon on the Mount, Jesus squarely addressed his followers' financial anxiety:

For this reason I say to you, do not be worried about your life, as to what you will eat or what you will drink; nor for your body, as to what you will put on. Is not life more than food, and the body more than clothing? Look at the birds of the air, that they do not sow, nor reap nor gather into barns, and yet your heavenly Father feeds them. Are you not worth much more than they? And who of you by being worried can add a single hour to his life? And why are you worried about clothing? Observe how the lilies of the field grow; they do not toil nor do they spin, yet I say to you that not even Solomon in all his glory clothed himself like one of these. But if God so clothes the grass of the field, which is alive today and tomorrow is thrown into the furnace, will he not much more clothe you? You of little faith! Do not worry then, saying, 'What will we eat?' or 'What will we drink?' or 'What will we wear for clothing?' For the Gentiles eagerly seek all these things; for your heavenly Father knows that you need all these things. But seek first his kingdom and his righteousness, and all these things will be added to you. So do not worry about tomorrow; for tomorrow will care for itself. Each day has enough trouble of its own. (Matthew 6:25-34)

Our worry is evidence that we don't really trust God. Genuine trust in a faithful God delivers the peace that money promises but can never provide.

James 2:5 reminds us that God chooses the poor of this earth to be rich in faith and heirs to an eternal kingdom. The poor are rich in faith because they have no other means by which to survive, and they experience the continuing joy of God's just-in-time provision.

What about the rich? The rich in James's day were oppressing the poor and dragging them into court; in so doing, they blasphemed the name of Christ. How are you using your wealth? As you read the news of the day, do you find yourself inevitably agreeing with the rich and powerful while feeling contempt for the poor? I have to constantly check my political positions against the word of God, remembering that my highest allegiance is not to the USA or to a political party, and certainly not to the rich and powerful of this earth, but to my heavenly Father. If he is my highest allegiance, I have to remember that my heavenly Father loves the poor because they so readily look to him for provision.

Who would you rather be: someone who's poor by worldly standards and yet rich in faith, or someone who's rich by worldly standards but with a thin faith and an easily deflated hope? Are you still trying to convince yourself that there's a both/and? There's an industry of teachers who sell exactly that idea, but I challenge you to test that teaching against the Scriptures I've presented in this chapter.

During my struggles after 2008, a friend gave me a document listing many of God's promises for provision, including the verses I recite in this chapter. Every day, I sat in my office and recited those verses aloud while I prayed for direction, for provision, and for hope. Many days, I literally lay face down on the floor of my office, prostrating myself before God as I desperately sought him. This practice didn't last for weeks or months, but for years. God heard me, he provided for me, and he richly blessed me beyond all I could have asked or imagined. I don't mean merely that he met my family's needs during the crisis; I mean that God changed my heart. I began to recognize the degree to which he is my sole source of provision. I began to experience a peace that was independent of the shifting sands of circumstance. I began to grow in these things, and I'm still growing. I wouldn't have grown in this way through uninterrupted prosperity.

In hindsight, I can say now that I'm profoundly grateful for the financial crisis of 2008. I grew in intimacy with my heavenly Father and he lifted the heavy burden of self-sufficiency from my shoulders. He placed another yoke on me, but Jesus's yoke is easy and his burden is light (Matthew 11:28-30).

God's kingdom includes both people who are rich and those who are poor on this earth. Many godly people use their wealth to serve that kingdom, and many poor people fail to serve that kingdom at all. Neither poverty nor wealth are virtues, but Scripture is clear that faith in money is idolatry, and avarice is an obstacle to spiritual maturity. Yet the heart of many Christians is more inclined toward accumulation of wealth than to submission to Christ.

God has chosen the poor of this earth to be rich in faith and heirs of the kingdom. Do you want to be among them, or would you rather be rich in the eyes of the world? This is the point at which many admit to themselves that they don't want to be a for-real Christian, because they've invested their hope too fully in money. You may be thinking, "Well yes, but..." as you formulate exceptions and qualifications to the concepts I've described here. We're well practiced in the apologetics of wealth.

My intention in this chapter is not to let the rich off the hook, because we rich generally let ourselves off the hook too easily. Let these truths simmer, and assess your heart in light of them. Bring everything you have and every hope you hold to the cross of Christ, and set them before him with abandon. In return, you'll inherit eternal treasure that moth and rust cannot destroy and thieves cannot break in and steal (Matthew 6:19-21).

Discussion Questions

1. What do you tend to ask for God to provide?
2. How should your requests be different?
3. What are some experiences where you've clearly seen God's provision?
4. Though we're not often lacking for food or shelter, how can we put ourselves in places of full reliance upon God for his kingdom rather than our own?

12

WE DON'T GET TO DEFINE SIN

If, however, you are fulfilling the royal law according to
the Scripture, "You shall love your neighbor as yourself,"
you are doing well. But if you show partiality, you are committing sin and are convicted by the law as transgressors.
For whoever keeps the whole law and yet stumbles in one point,
he has become guilty of all. For he who said "Do not commit
adultery," also said, "Do not commit murder." Now if you
do not commit adultery, but do commit murder,
you have become a transgressor of the law.

JAMES 2:8-11

I was on a roll. I was holding court amid friends while condemn-
ing the evils of legalism. I was quoting some of my favorite
verses about Christian liberty and telling clever jokes about
Christians who created extrabiblical rules and used them to burden others. I would probably have been even more persuasive if
I weren't slurring my words, because I'd had too much to drink.
I was in the midst of committing a favored sin while criticizing
a sin I despised. But I don't get to decide what is and what isn't

sin. Unless Scripture defines sin for me, my concept of sin will be nothing other than a projection of my personal preferences.

Most of us have a natural inclination to ignore or minimize our own sin while easily spotting sin in others. This attitude fuels self-righteousness, inhibits our intimacy with God, and factures our relationships with brothers and sisters in Christ. This attitude also fails to acknowledge our desperate and shared need for a Savior. Most of us treat wealthy people differently than we treat homeless people, and we don't think it's a big deal, but James tells us that partiality is a sin. It's no less a sin than legalism, drunkenness, sexual immorality, or other things we more readily condemn.

Throughout history, man has sought to define sin in a way that suits him. A person prone to zeal is inclined to condemn the peacemaker for being passive, while the peacemaker is inclined to condemn the zealous man as divisive. The glutton condemns the sexually immoral, the sexually immoral condemn the greedy, the greedy condemns the slothful, the slothful condemns the drunkard, the drunkard condemns the legalist. And so it goes—we're quick to label and slow to repent, more concerned about where others fail than about repenting from our own sinful behavior.

We don't get to define sin. The true definition of sin doesn't change with time or fashions. God defines sin in his word to us, and any sin is sufficient to separate us from God—except that Christ's atoning sacrifice is sufficient to satisfy it all. Showing partiality is a sin, and many of us are guilty of it. Partiality is a sin because it's a failure to love others as God calls us to love.

James 2:8 speaks of the "royal law," which means that this law is supreme or binding. Jesus defined this law for us when a scholar asked him to identify the greatest commandment.

Jesus responded with two: to love God and to love one another (Matthew 22:36-40). God's highest and greatest commands are that we love. What does this tell us about God's character? The apostle John writes, "The one who does not love does not know God, for God is love" (1 John 4:8). Any Christian who dismisses an emphasis on love as soft sentimentality is ignoring the vast weight of Scripture. Jesus himself said:

> If you keep my commandments, you will abide in My love; just as I have kept my Father's commandments and abide in his love. These things I have spoken to you so that My joy may be in you, and that your joy may be made full. This is my commandment, that you love one another, just as I have loved you. Greater love has no one than this, that one lay down his life for his friends. (John 15:10-13)

Why is the sin of personal favoritism such a big deal? James anticipates the question. He knows we'll be inclined either to reject favoritism as an actual sin, or to consider it a sin of minimal importance. (We do this with many sins, either because we personally struggle to avoid them or because our culture has ceased to recognize them as sin.) James explains that favoritism is a gross sin because it's a failure to love, and if we sin in the area of favoritism, we're guilty of breaking the whole law.

Favoritism was so normal for James's original readers that they failed to recognize it as sin. I suggest we're no different today, not only concerning personal favoritism but also many other patterns of behavior that are displeasing to God. Are we in the evangelical church as concerned about favoritism, greed, worry, or gluttony as we are about sexual sin? Were you shocked at the start of this chapter to read my confession of the sin of drunkenness, yet unconcerned about your own gossip, gluttony, or greed? Are we making false distinctions between our own sin and the sin we easily criticize in those around us?

Before we proceed, allow me to clarify one thing. I've heard many say that all sins are equal in God's sight, or that no one sin is greater than another. But there are greatly varying natural consequences between, for example, stealing your neighbor's newspaper and murdering your neighbor. Both are sins, but they have very different natural consequences, both for the person sinned against and for the sinner. God's law as revealed in the Old Testament demonstrates that God considered some sins more grievous than other sins. In Proverbs 6:16-19, Solomon singles out seven sins that God considers abominable: (1) pride and conceit, (2) lying and falsehood, (3) shedding of innocent blood, (4) wicked, scheming hearts, (5) the pursuit of evil, (6) false testimony, and (7) dissension and conflicts. We might be surprised at some of these, but they support the idea that some sins are more grievous than other sins in God's sight. The apostle Paul emphasized the unique destructiveness of sexual sin. He described sexual sin as a sin against our own body, as opposed to other sins outside the body (1 Corinthians 6:18). Those of us who've had to recover from sexual sin know that sexual sin cuts deep and leaves lasting wounds. James isn't saying all sin is the same, or that all sin leads to the same natural consequences.

If not all sins are equal, what does James mean when he says that one who stumbles at one point of the law is guilty of having broken it all? He means that God is a holy God, and that any single sin is sufficient to separate us from him and to deny us a place at his side for eternity. The only salvation from judgment is to believe in and confess the atoning sacrifice and resurrection of Jesus our Lord, God's only Son. There's no weighing of good deeds versus bad deeds to determine whether we've won entry into heaven. There is but one way—and that way is Jesus.

Therein lies the gravity of the sin of personal favoritism. Favoritism denies our universally shared need for a Savior. The rich have no less need for salvation than the poor. And the rich have no greater standing in the kingdom of God than the poor. By ranking one another based on financial or social standing, we deny the essential truth of our equal footing before God.

You might be asking, "What's love got to do with it? Why does James introduce this section about partiality by talking about love?" James includes this command because it's impossible to love others if we condition our love on status. In an atmosphere of personal favoritism, even our love for the rich is not the sort of love God requires, because a love based on personal favoritism is inherently selfish, premised on what we might get out of the relationship and the advantages to be gained from associating with a wealthy person.

If we fulfill the royal law by loving one another as we love ourselves, we're doing well. This isn't easy, but it also isn't complicated. Loving one another involves a dying to self, and a surrender of our personal ambitions to the will of God. It's impossible to love well when we view the objects of our love as being somehow inferior to ourselves. Acts stemming from an attitude of favoritism have more to do with serving our own egos than Christian love. James is calling us to a higher love, a love imitating the love Christ has shown for us. God gives his love not to the deserving, the accomplished, the prosperous, or the brilliant, but to all who seek him.

God's word tells us that favoritism is a sin. It's a nearly universal sin, and one that's difficult to avoid, but we're wrong to think it's not a sin. Our calling is to obey. Consider, for just a moment, how Christ-glorifying it would if his followers would love without favoritism. The world would change.

Discussion Questions

1. How did reading this chapter impact you? What are some of your initial responses?
2. What points in this chapter struck you as compelling or personally challenging?
3. How have you seen or personally experienced the sin of partiality affecting the body of Christ, or affecting your own life?
4. For a person experiencing conviction in this area, what might repentance look like?
5. We've seen how the sin of partiality is in many ways a culturally accepted practice among believers today. In order for this not to be true of the next generation of the church, what must happen in the body of Christ now?

13

THE LAW
OF LIBERTY

So speak and so act as those who are to be judged by
the law of liberty. For judgment will be merciless
to one who has shown no mercy;
mercy triumphs over judgment.

JAMES 2:12-13

ercy triumphs over judgment. It's sadly ironic that this beautiful and victorious truth, the very foundation of our faith, causes as much consternation as it does rejoicing. Too many of us become Pharisees in the face of this truth, clinging to our favored set of laws instead of embracing the liberating truth that we're free in Christ. Like joyless scolds, we fret about what Christians might do if this concept is "over-taught," when in fact this teaching should be at the forefront of all that we speak. If mercy hadn't triumphed over judgment, there would be no gospel to preach.

James begins this passage (2:12-13) with "So," prompting us to consider what preceded it. The whole of chapter 2 leading up to these verses is devoted to the noxious sin of personal favoritism.

THE LAW OF LIBERTY

Partiality in the church is a particularly grievous sin because it reveals a belief that wealth and high status are valid ways to measure a man. When we treat rich people better than we treat poor people, we're viewing people through the prism of wealth rather than of grace. This is why James begins chapter 2 with "Do not hold your faith...with an attitude of personal favoritism." Instead of holding our faith with an attitude of favoritism, we're to speak and act as those who are to be judged by the law of liberty, the same law that James told his readers (in 1:25) to look at intently and abide by.

So what is this perfect law of liberty?

The phrase "law of liberty" may seem oxymoronic. Law creates barriers, while liberty removes them. Paul himself associates the law with slavery and condemnation (Galatians 4; 2 Corinthians 3:9) while associating liberty with the Spirit of God and with freedom (2 Corinthians 3:17, Galatians 5:1). But law and liberty are contradictory only if we understand the law in the limited sense of rules governing conduct, such as those included in the Old Testament Mosaic law.

Nomos, the Greek term for law that James uses, is elastic—similar to the English word "law." *Nomos* can describe statutes, but it also describes principles and natural forces or permanent truths.[25] Paul writes of a new sort of law, the "law of faith" by which we're justified to God (Romans 3:27). Paul describes this overarching law as "the law of the Spirit of life in Christ Jesus" (Romans 8:2). This is the law James is referring to here—the law of the gospel of Jesus Christ.

What does it mean to be judged by this law? It means that each of us will be judged based on a single question: Is our name written in the Book of Life (Revelation 20:11-15)? Our names are written in this book if the Spirit of God dwells within us (Romans 8). The Spirit dwells within God's children (Galatians

4:6), and we're God's adopted children if we have faith in Christ Jesus (Galatians 3:26). Our salvation is based on the accomplished work of Jesus Christ. We'll be judged on whether we've received this gift, not on any performance standard. We're set free from the law of sin and death (Romans 8:2).

This is a glorious truth, a liberating truth! But we view it with skepticism. It's contrary to the familiar system of this world—where we perform and we win, or we fail and we lose. As brutal as this earthly system is, we find it comfortable because it gives us the illusion of control. God calls us to a truth so otherworldly, and so utterly dependent on his goodness and mercy, that we struggle to process it. Rather than embrace the law of liberty, we become like the elder brother Jesus spoke of (in Luke 15:11-32), who seethes while his prodigal younger brother enjoys his good father's embrace. Or we're like the laborer hired at dawn who's now chafing because the laborer hired in the late afternoon receives equal pay (Matthew 20:1-16)—why should our decades of relative morality be rewarded the same as the long life lived in sin before an eleventh-hour conversion?

Our fleshly impulse is to earn and to deserve, and we struggle to receive the gift freely given. This is a variation of the sin in the garden of Eden, where Eve rejected dependence on God to become her own god. Our salvation comes from Christ's work and his grace, not from our own working. If we don't accept this essential truth, our joy will be forever tepid, we'll struggle with self-righteousness, and we'll risk missing the very thing we're seeking to earn.

How do we speak and act as someone who'll be judged by this "law of liberty," this principle that Christ saves us according to his grace and not according to our merit? We live a life without favoritism and full of forgiveness and mercy. If we all stand or fall based on the accomplished work of our risen Lord rather than our own works, what room is there for pride? A self-righteous, haughty spirit is completely inconsistent with this law of liberty. This is why James writes, "Judgment will be merciless to one who has shown no mercy."

Jesus himself emphasized the evil of failing to forgive. He tells the parable of a servant whose master graciously forgave his steward an impossibly massive debt (Matthew 18:21-35), yet that same steward then refused to forgive a much smaller debt. The master heard of this and handed the unforgiving steward over to torturers until he could repay the debt, which would be never—it's a description of hell. Similarly, in the Sermon on the Mount, when Jesus taught his disciples to pray "Forgive us our debts as we also have forgiven our debtors," he gave this explanation: "For if you forgive others for their transgressions, your heavenly Father will also forgive you. But if you do not forgive others, then your Father will not forgive your transgressions" (Matthew 6:12-15). There's an uncomfortable conditionality in these verses, and when Scripture is uncomfortable, we tend to explain it into irrelevance. Don't do that here. This truth should be so uncomfortable that it changes us—that's the point. We all stand in the position of the steward in that we've been forgiven an unpayable debt. Do we extend a similar mercy to others?

If you're worried about any moral anarchy that might come from the triumph of mercy over judgment, consider the work of the Spirit of God. We are, in the working of our own flesh, incapable of living a godly life. At its very best, fleshly effort accomplishes a superficial and inconsistent morality that masks a discontented and independent heart. But when we're fully submitted to God in joyful dependence, his Spirit works mightily in us. Our life bears the natural fruit of that Spirit, which is love, joy, peace, patience, kindness, goodness, faithfulness, gentleness, and self-control (Galatians 5:22-23). A person submitted to God bears this good fruit as naturally as he breathes. This is what it looks like to so speak and so act as one who'll be judged by the law of liberty.

We aren't called to be the morality police for a fallen world. We're called to make disciples of Jesus Christ. If moral conduct holds a more prominent place in our theology than grace, we've missed the gospel entirely.

Mercy triumphs over judgment. In the shadow of this glorious truth, favoritism based on the trivial hierarchies of this fallen world should disappear. This isn't a scriptural problem to explain, but a glorious truth to embrace.

Discussion Questions

1. Before reading this chapter, if someone had asked you to explain the relationship between forgiveness and mercy, how would you have answered?

2. Describe an instance where you've experienced forgiveness with mercy—either as the recipient or as the giver.

3. How have you personally seen or experienced the truth that "mercy triumphs over judgment" (James 2:13)?

14

A USEFUL FAITH

What use is it, my brethren, if someone says he has faith but
he has no works? Can that faith save him? If a brother or sister is
without clothing and in need of daily food, and one of you says
to them, "Go in peace, be warmed and be filled," and yet you do
not give them what is necessary for their body, what use is that?
Even so faith, if it has no works, is dead, being by itself.
But someone may well say, "You have faith and I have works;
show me your faith without the works, and I will show you my
faith by my works." You believe that God is one. You do well;
the demons also believe, and shudder. But are you willing to
recognize, you foolish fellow, that faith without works is useless?
Was not Abraham our father justified by works when he offered
up Isaac his son on the altar? You see that faith was working with
his works, and as a result of the works, faith was perfected; and
the Scripture was fulfilled which says, "And Abraham believed
God, and it was reckoned to him as righteousness," and he was
called the friend of God. You see that a man is justified by works
and not by faith alone. In the same way, was not Rahab the harlot
also justified by works when she received the messengers and
sent them out by another way? For just as the body without the
spirit is dead, so also faith without works is dead.

James 2:14-26

've taught an adult Sunday school class at my church for many years. One Sunday morning, I stood at my familiar podium in front of friendly faces, but my stomach was aflutter. I felt a little bit sick, and really didn't want to be there at all. I was teaching on Ephesians 6:1, which reads, "Children, obey your parents in the Lord, for this is right." My lesson included the following sentences:

> A child who grows up not knowing how to obey their parents will struggle to obey God. A child who is trained to obey only when it seems reasonable or rational to them will not learn to obey God when his plans aren't matching up with their finite understanding. A child who learns obedience to their parents will more easily align their behavior to God's calling and commands even when it seems hard or when the reasons are not altogether clear.

Why was I so nervous? Because that very week, we'd caught our eldest son, a high school sophomore, doing drugs.[26] This was devastating. I thought I'd done all the right things as a parent. My son had been in church nearly every week of his life, and we taught the word of God in our home. I'd taught him to take care of the yard, coached his teams, and spent untold weekends with him in the woods, pouring God's truth into his young mind while teaching him to backpack and hunt. I thought I was a good dad. Now he was not only disobeying, but also overtly denying Christ. Yet there I stood that morning, called upon to teach on parenting when I'd failed as a parent.

Frankly, I was disappointed with God. I felt that I'd done my part, but God had let me down. I thought that with proper input, I'd get predictable output. How could I teach a lesson on a child's obedience when my own child was in rebellion? The fact that I was scheduled to teach on this particular passage that week seemed a divine cruelty. God's word also says, "Train up a child in the way he should go. Even when he is old, he will not depart from it" (Proverbs 22:6). Did I still believe this? When my experience wasn't matching up with God's promises, how could I stand there and teach? I had to decide: Would I teach in faith, believing God's word and his promises despite what was in front of me? I felt like I was stepping over an abyss. Would God support my foot if I stepped out in faith?

Martin Luther once described James as a "right strawy epistle."[27] I'm not altogether sure what "strawy" means, but it's safe to say that James wasn't Luther's favorite book in the Bible. This is primarily because of the passage I'm writing about in this chapter. Luther's phrase *sola fide*, which means "by faith alone," was one of the driving concepts of the Reformation, and today remains the chief distinctive between the Roman Catholic and Protestant faiths. In debate, Catholics point out that the only place in Scripture where the phrase "faith alone" appears is here in James 2:24, which reads, "A man is justified by works and *not* by faith alone."

There's an apparent tension between James's words in 2:24 and several Pauline passages, including these: "For by grace you have been saved through faith; and that not of yourselves, it's the gift of God, not as a result of works" (Ephesians 2:8-9); "For we maintain that a man is justified by faith apart from works" (Romans 3:28); "But to the one who does not work, but believes in him who justifies the ungodly, his faith is credited as righteousness" (Romans 4:5); "But if it is by grace, it is no longer on the basis of works, otherwise grace is no longer grace" (Romans 11:6); "Does he who provides you with the Spirit and works miracles among you, do it by the works of the Law, or by hearing with faith?" (Galatians 3:5-6).

The theology of *sola fide* is well supported in Scripture, so what do we do with this passage in James? Do we, like Luther, wish it away? Alternatively, do we grieve over an apparent contradiction in Scripture? Let's instead probe a little deeper, and we'll discover a truth that can enrich our relationship with God, exhort us on to a surer walk with Christ, and bless us with a more useful faith.

The Greek word translated here as "faith" is *pistis,* which means "a firm persuasion, a conviction based upon hearing."[28] New Testament writers always use the word in reference to faith in God or Christ.[29] The Greek word *ergon,* translated here as "works," denotes an employment or task; it's simply something that we do.[30]

Note how James starts this passage: "What *use* is it, my brethren, if someone says he has faith but he has no works." Later, in 2:20, he writes, "Faith without works is *useless.*" James is writing to people who profess belief in Jesus; his emphasis in this letter is the walking out of that belief, not the attainment of it. As twenty-first-century Christians, we tend to think the Bible always refers to eternal salvation when the word "saved" is used, but the Bible's writers often meant other things—such as being saved from physical death, saved from a lesser life, or saved from a useless and ineffective walk in Christ. James's words here apply to us all. Our lack of works may evidence a weak or immature faith resulting in a useless life, albeit one that will see heaven at its earthly end. On the other hand, our lack of works may evidence our total lack of true faith—resulting in a life that ends in hell.

What God desires in us is not merely correct doctrine, even if sincerely held. God desires our obedience and trust. James says that even demons are monotheists, but that doesn't mean they're heirs to God's kingdom. Satan knows who God is and who God's

Son is; he knows also that humanity's salvation comes through God's Son. But Satan refused to submit to God and forfeited his place in heaven, even though his doctrinal understanding was accurate. Correct doctrine is not equivalent to true faith. True faith is always evidenced by a changed life. As Warren Wiersbe said, "Hearing God's word and talking about God's word can never substitute for doing God's word."[31]

You could easily misconstrue my next point if I'm not careful. So let me preface this by confirming that God calls Christians to do good works. James reminded us in his letter's first chapter that pure and undefiled religion in the sight of God is visiting widows and orphans in their distress. Paul says we should walk in a manner worthy of the Lord, bearing fruit in good works (Colossians 1:10). Scripture is abundantly clear that Christians should be engaged in good works in the sense of helping the poor and oppressed. People should know Christians for their good works, and doing good works is an important part of walking out the Christian faith. But I don't believe that James's discussion of "works" here addresses good works as we normally understand them. Instead, I think James is referring to what I call "faith works."

"Good works" are acts of benevolence that almost everyone recognizes as good. "Faith works," as I use the phrase here, are things that people do only because they actually believe the words of God spoken in Scripture. A faith work is something that can succeed only if God shows up, something we couldn't accomplish through our effort and planning alone. God calls us elsewhere to good works, but I think that James here is discussing "faith works" instead.

James's story about sending away the brother in need is an analogy explaining the uselessness of faith that's not evidenced by works. A person who says to the needy, "Go in peace, be warmed and be filled," but doesn't actually help has been useless to the needy person. Similarly, if we don't perform "faith works" that evidence trust in God, our verbal expressions of faith are hollow and useless.

James provides two examples of "faith works": Abraham's interrupted sacrifice of Isaac on the altar, and Rahab's conspiring with the Hebrew spies in Jericho. Neither sacrificing your child nor betraying your country are "good works" in the sense I describe above. They are, however, "faith works" that neither Abraham nor Rahab would have done unless they genuinely believed in God. Abraham received unequivocal instruction from God that made absolutely no sense at all, but he obeyed. Rahab had heard the stories of the Hebrew God delivering his people from Egypt, and she believed in this God enough to place all her bets entirely on him. God rewarded both Abraham and Rahab for their faith. God delivered a substitute sacrifice for Abraham's son Isaac (foreshadowing Jesus's substitutionary sacrifice on our behalf). Consequently, Isaac became the father of a nation and a direct ancestor of Jesus. Rahab, who also appears in Christ's genealogy, saved herself and her family from death while also playing a role in delivering God's people into the Promised Land.

James says that Abraham was called a "friend of God." Abraham believed in God's character and in the efficacy of God's promises. When Abraham acted on his faith, his faith was perfected in the sense of being completed or evidenced. So too, when we choose courses of action that make sense only if we believe, our faith is also perfected. When our faith is perfected by actual exercise of that faith, we walk more closely with God and live more useful lives of faith. Working in faith begets more faith.

Why did James use Rahab as an example of faith rather than a more obviously noble character like Noah, Samuel, Elijah, or

Daniel? In many respects, Rahab is an unlikely choice. She wasn't an example of moral works righteousness, she wasn't an adherent of the law, and she wasn't even a Hebrew. She is, however, included in both the genealogy of Jesus (Matthew 1:5) and the list in Hebrews 11 of persons having great faith (11:31). I think James chose to mention Rahab—an unlikely paragon of faith—to help clarify that a perfected faith isn't the same as a perfect moral character. Perfected faith is a faith evidenced by action.

Rahab's story is contained in Joshua 2, where she hid and assisted Hebrew spies in Jericho. The Jewish hero Joshua, successor to Moses, was preparing the Hebrew army for an invasion of Canaan, and Jericho stood in the way. He sent the spies into Jericho to help plan the attack. The guards in Jericho heard about the presence of the spies and came looking for them at Rahab's brothel, but she hid the spies and lied to the guards. Once the guards left her brothel, she made the spies promise to spare her and her family in the coming conquest. What if Rahab had said, "I believe in your God," but then handed the spies over to the guards? She could have justified it: "Well, if God can do anything, then he can deliver those spies. I'm just being practical and responsible." How would we have known that her belief in a God she couldn't see was real—and how would Rahab have known—unless she chose to trust in him instead of in the strength of her city's walls? Rahab's "work" was an affirmative act of belief that perfected her faith. Her faith was extremely risky—and the only means for her salvation. The alternative was death.

In a for-real Christian's life, the numbers often don't add up, the decisions often don't make sense, and the outcomes often defy earthly expectations. Abraham's act of offering up Isaac and Rahab's act of hiding the spies made no sense except that both Abraham and Rahab believed in the goodness and greatness of a

God they couldn't see. What we often seek is the easily accounted for life where we experience the predictable outcomes of logical decision-making in order to avoid suffering. But the author of Hebrews says that faith is being assured of things hoped for (things we don't yet have), and being convinced of things we don't see (Hebrews 11:1). The Bible promises a peace that passes all understanding (Philippians 4:7). Yet what we prefer is a peace that's perfectly understandable because it comes from pleasant circumstances. The perfectly understandable life is not the life of faith. Are we willing to live the life for which there is no accounting?

Many have used this passage to argue that we need to take care of the poor in order to evidence a true saving faith. But writing a check or serving in a soup kitchen are things we can easily accomplish without trusting in God. James is exhorting his readers to engage in "faith works." If James were emphasizing acts of charity, he would have focused on other examples than Abraham and Rahab. James is warning Christians against living useless lives where works of faith are absent. He's exhorting us to complete our faith in God by doing things that make sense only because we believe God is real and God is good. The for-real Christian reacts, decides, and endures in ways that non-Christians find inexplicable.

Now, back to that Sunday school podium years ago. I stepped out in faith and taught my lesson. My voice quavered and I cried in front of my class. I hate to cry, and I particularly hate to cry in public. I taught God's truth even while revealing my broken heart. The moment crushed my pride, and this was a good thing. I was suffering. Without knowing exactly why I was in distress, my class had compassion on me and prayed for me. Notwithstanding what was in front of me, I chose to believe in the eternal truth of God's word and stepped out in faith.

Some months after I gave that lesson, my son gave his life to the Lord (due to the influence of others; God was showing me that he is sovereign and I am not), and I participated in his baptism. Since then, I've rejoiced to witness his growing in grace and godly wisdom. Recently, he gave his testimony in front of a gathering of men. His testimony, in all its detail, mortifies my flesh and exalts God. This is a good thing. I know that not everyone's story (including my own) is quite as tidy as my son's journey to faith. But even when life is messy—especially then—God calls us to step out in faith when circumstances suggest we should retreat. It's in those moments that God shows up, and our faith is perfected.

We Christians say we believe in an all-powerful God who created the universe. We claim that Jesus is God incarnate, personifying God's word to us (John 1:15). We profess that Jesus lived a perfect life, then gave his very life as the perfect and final atonement for our sins. We proclaim that Jesus bodily rose from the dead in a magnificent conquest over sin and death. That same Jesus called us to stop storing up our treasures on earth and to start storing them up in heaven, to stop hating and start loving, to stop coveting and start being grateful. He told us to stop committing acts of sexual immorality, to give to the poor, and to stop worrying. He told us to seek his kingdom first, and to make his truth the very foundation of our lives.[32] To do these things is costly, and it requires genuine trust. If we say we believe in this magnificent Jesus, but fail to do the things he tells us to do—do we really believe at all? James says no.

Have you been stuck in discouragement and spiritual depression? Has your faith felt dead? If a man says he has faith, but he has no works, can such a faith save him from that life? God is calling you to do something that makes no sense unless he is real. It could be a confession, a repentance, a surrender of control, or a giving away of your money. It may be as simple as joining a small group or waking up an hour earlier in the morning to spend time in God's word. It may be as radical as falling to your knees right now in repentance, confessing that you haven't really believed until now, and you now want to live a life of real faith. Do it—now! You have no idea what today will bring.

Hiding the spies was risky, but it was Rahab's only path to life. Likewise, the only path away from a useless life of dead faith is the one that evidences our complete trust God. Live the kind of life for which there's no earthly explanation.

Discussion Questions:

1. What is something you read in this chapter that left an impression on you, or challenged you to live a life of faith?
2. Why do you think James chose Abraham and Rahab to illustrate his message, when he could have picked from so many other Old Testament people who made obedient, moral choices?
3. Stepping out in faith often produces even more faith. Can you think of a time when you experienced this to be true?
4. Is there a difference between (a) following God out of obedience, and (b) following God because you trust in his character and promises? If so, what is it?

15

TOO MANY TEACHERS

Let not many of you become teachers, my brethren,
knowing that as such we will incur a stricter judgment.
For we all stumble in many ways.
If anyone does not stumble in what he says,
he is a perfect man, able to bridle the whole body as well.

JAMES 3:1-2

This chapter has been difficult for me to write, because I'm a teacher. James aims his warning squarely at me, and I struggle to discuss these verses in a way that's neither self-glorifying nor self-condemning. I'm an attorney by vocation, but I've also served as a teacher of God's word for my entire adult life—to young children, teenagers, and adults. To serve as a teacher is both a great honor and a great responsibility to which not many are called.

James wasn't speaking here of parents teaching their children, or a master teaching an apprentice, or a schoolteacher with students.[33] James was speaking specifically to people who taught God's word. In the days of the synagogue system, which the early church emulated, virtually any man in the congregation could stand and address the assembly.[34] Such men obviously had varying ability and disparate motives in doing so. James is saying (in 3:12) that only those who are equipped and capable of teaching God's word should teach.

The church body needs teachers, and so God bestows the gift of teaching upon certain people (Romans 12:7; 1 Corinthians 12:28; Ephesians 4:11). However, in Paul's description of spiritual gifts, he points out that not every believer holds every gift: "All are not teachers, are they?" (1 Corinthians 12:29). As a church, we ignore both Paul and James when we place those not gifted as teachers in teaching roles. Individuals who aren't gifted to teach ignore those warnings when they seek a teaching role rather than the role for which they've been gifted. This error is understandable, because we tend to esteem the teaching gift above other gifts. We therefore need to grow in our appreciation of the other gifts.

I've discovered that my effectiveness as a teacher is very limited unless I work with people who are leaders, givers, and exhorters—all gifts that I don't have. The gifted servant who arrives at church early to make coffee and set up chairs should be no less esteemed than the teacher. The body of Christ works best when we encourage people to serve in the roles for which they're gifted.

Many years ago, I took a spiritual gift assessment at church. The results indicated that I had the gift of mercy. I told my wife, "I hate my spiritual gift. From what I can tell, it just means I have to take a lot of crap from people without complaining about it." My wife wisely said, "I don't think you have the gift of mercy." Since then, I've grown in my appreciation of that gift, even as I've realized I don't have it.

Don't assume you have the gift of teaching just because your church asks you to teach. There are many mature Christians who know and love God's word, but whose gifting is in other areas.

How then do we determine whether someone is gifted to teach? We should ask whether they've demonstrated a love for the Bible as evidenced by diligent study, whether their teachings flow from the word of God rather than their own opinion or agenda, whether they honestly present the word without manipulation, whether they're capable of clearly communicating the truths of God's word rather than creating confusion, and whether their lives reflect what they're teaching.

There's a difference between being a talented speaker and a gifted teacher. Some charismatic speakers are spiritual charlatans who seek the role of teacher in an effort to enhance their prestige or fill their pockets. On the other hand, there are many gifted spiritual teachers whose speaking style won't draw crowds, but who faithfully exercise their gift in the smaller settings God has provided. When we walk away from a true teacher's teaching, we should be edified, equipped, exhorted, and enriched in truth rather than merely entertained. Rather than remembering the speaker, we should remember the truths taught. Too many churches and Christian organizations have gone astray by relying on the charisma of a speaker rather than the truth of the Bible as the basis for their ministry.

James tells us that not many should aspire to be teachers because teachers will be held to a stricter judgment. As a teacher, this is sobering to me, as it should be. In comparison with those who don't serve as teachers, my speech should be more seasoned with grace, and my conduct more above reproach. I'm mindful of Jesus's teaching in Matthew that "whoever causes one of these little ones who believe in me to stumble, it would be better for him to have a millstone hung around his neck, and to be drowned in the depths of the sea" (Matthew 18:6). The salvation of a believing teacher is not imperiled because he makes a mistake as a teacher, but false teachers can expect a future judgment—believers with respect to reward (1 Corinthians 4:3-5), and nonbelievers with respect to punishment (Jude 14-15). God also disciplines false teachers in this life in order to limit the effects of their teaching. We've seen many humiliating public falls of false teachers, which is the intervention of God.

James 3:2 explains why it's so challenging to be a good teacher. Teaching, more than most gifts, utilizes the untamable tongue. I'm forever amazed at the ways in which my tongue gets me into trouble. Just one careless phrase from the podium of my Sunday school class can cause great confusion or discouragement. One careless click of the "Post" button on Facebook in a moment of anger can set my community on fire. Because I valued my teaching gift too little when I was younger, I failed to appreciate the impact my words had on many people. It was only after some years of teaching that I came to recognize the effect of my words on my listeners, for good or for ill. This is true of both my carefully prepared lessons and my careless, casual comments. I'm still growing in this discipline.

Most sobering of all, the quality of my teaching springs from the state of my heart. When I'm walking rightly with God, my words ring with authority and power because they flow from alignment with the word of God. When I'm drifting in my walk, my words may be correct, but they take on the quality of a liturgical recitation in a dead church—accurate but heartless. When my words are both true and powerful, they reflect my submission to the God who places those words on my heart.

My most powerful teaching doesn't flow from experiences where I've prospered, or from any notably good deeds on my part (which would be a limited inventory indeed). My most powerful teaching flows from pain, embarrassment, fear, confessed sin, and wrestling through doubts and questions (of which there's no shortage of stories). This can be frustrating to me, because God will often have me struggle through something that's apropos to what I'll soon be teaching. Sometimes that makes me want to quit teaching. I don't like to suffer, but cannot escape the fact that others are often blessed through my suffering. This repeated process now causes me to view suffering through a different lens.

Pride is one of the greatest temptations we teachers face. If we're faithfully teaching God's word, this often results in adulation, because lives are changing under our teaching. The word of God does not return void (Isaiah 55:11). We teachers must remember that our teaching's power stems not from our flesh or merit, but from the eternal truth and glorious power of the gospel we're privileged to proclaim. The moment we believe otherwise, we're in great peril. Yet we teachers also struggle with discouragement when we don't see good fruit from our teaching. In those moments, we must remember that our ministries are not about elevating our self-esteem but about glorifying the God who's responsible for the fruit. My prayer as a teacher is that I'll receive enough encouragement to insulate me from despair, but never so much that I'm tempted to pride.

For-real Christians identify their spiritual gift and employ it in serving the kingdom of God, whether that gift is teaching, serving, encouraging, giving, or something else. James considered himself a teacher, saying, "*We* will incur a stricter judgment." He personally understood both the rewards and dangers of teaching. Don't view his words as a prohibition, or even a discouragement for those gifted to teach. However, not many should aspire to the role. Those hoping to enhance their status or line their pockets shouldn't seek to teach. Those who are teachers should be mindful of their tongues, which are ungovernable unless their lives are set in order beneath God's authority.

Discussion Questions:

1. If you were asked to accept a teaching role in your church or in a ministry—such as being a Sunday school teacher or small group leader—what affect would James 3:1 have on your decision about accepting that role?

2. Think of the most impactful teachers you've encountered. What traits did they share, and what made their teaching impactful for you? Do you share these traits?

3. For believers, our appearance before Christ's judgment seat (Greek *bema*, 2 Corinthians 5:10) will result in rewards for how we've lived. How much does this motivate you in how you live your life? What this either difficult or easy as a motivation for you?

16

THE UNTAMABLE TONGUE

Now if we put the bits into the horses' mouths so that
they will obey us, we direct their entire body as well. Look at
the ships also, though they are so great and are driven by strong
winds, are still directed by a very small rudder wherever the
inclination of the pilot desires. So also the tongue is a small part
of the body, and yet it boasts of great things. See how great
a forest is set aflame by such a small fire! And the tongue is a fire,
the very world of iniquity; the tongue is set among our members
as that which defiles the entire body, and sets on fire the course
of our life, and is set on fire by hell. For every species of beasts
and birds, of reptiles and creatures of the sea, is tamed and has
been tamed by the human race. But no one can tame the tongue;
it is a restless evil and full of deadly poison. With it we bless our
Lord and Father, and with it we curse men, who have been made
in the likeness of God; from the same mouth come both blessing
and cursing. My brethren, these things ought not to be this way.
Does a fountain send out from the same opening both fresh
and bitter water? Can a fig tree, my brethren, produce olives,
or a vine produce figs? Nor can salt water produce fresh.

JAMES 3:3-12

I enjoyed my friends' laughter as I sat at my college dining hall table. I was telling funny stories and relished being the center of attention. However, their responses grew more muted as I shifted to an embarrassing story about a classmate. When my story reached its crescendo, I was disappointed in the tepid response—only then noticing that the story's subject sat at the end of the table, having heard every embarrassing thing I'd said about him.

There are many such stories in my life that I wish I didn't remember, because when I do, I wince with regret. I wish I could go back in time and undo those moments. I'll sometimes wake up at night with a jolt after dreaming about a memory that produces intense guilt. I remember moments when I hurt someone, or shaded the truth, or sought to elevate myself at someone else's expense, or embarrassed others or myself. Almost all those moments involve something I've said—things that are imprudent, untrue, malicious, gossipy, cruel, or crude. Too many times I walk away from a conversation and immediately feel the taint of having said something I shouldn't have—an arrogant claim, a misdirected effort at humor, or a betrayal of a confidence. My unwise speech comes in many forms.

If I can derive any comfort from James's warning about the tongue in 3:3-12, it's in the fact that I'm clearly not alone. But his intention is not to comfort us. This is a dire warning, and one we often fail to heed. The tongue is an untamable beast, wreaking havoc in our relationships and causing untold damage within the church.

James begins chapter 3 with a warning to teachers, which is appropriate, since teachers' words carry particular power and potential to damage. But none of us are exempt from this warning about the tongue. With very few exceptions, we all speak. We tend to think of words as small things; after all, they have no physical substance and require little effort to produce. James corrects our perspective by identifying two other small things—the bit in a horse's mouth and a ship's rudder—having tremendous power to set the course of something much larger. The slight application of pressure on either of these small things changes the course of the apparently much more powerful thing. Similarly, a single tongue and the words it produces can change the course of many lives.

In the middle of 3:5, James changes his analogy. He begins by comparing the tongue to powerful things that are untamable. He equates the tongue with fire. Every summer we hear of wildfires raging in the western United States. These wildfires, usually started by a single lightning strike or a tiny match, consume hundreds of thousands of acres, killing wildlife, destroying precious habitats, and claiming hundreds of homes. It's heartbreaking to watch the footage of these out-of-control fires, seemingly unstoppable. For all his technical prowess, man has yet to tame fire. Every few blocks in our cities, there are fire stations full of brave men and women dedicated to stopping the spread, but they cannot prevent fire's destruction entirely. Similarly, a single unwise phrase can ignite unneeded controversy, consume communities, kill reputations, destroy peace, and claim families.

In 3:7, James compares the tongue to a wild beast. Many of us have visceral fears of certain types of animals, especially snakes. Snakes are difficult to see; we can step on or near them without knowing it, and some strike with deadly venom. Similarly, in an instant we can utter a careless word that acts as a deadly poison.

My wife is afraid of bears. Whenever we're in a wilderness park and crowds gather to watch a bear, she moves in the other direction—discretion outweighing curiosity. This is rational, because bears can act with tremendous force and wreak deadly havoc when they choose to attack. Yet many of us have seen trained serpents, bears, killer whales, and other beasts. James had seen similar things; he noted that though man can tame these mighty beasts, he hasn't been able to tame the tongue.

This passage is a challenge because James doesn't give any instruction on how we can tame the destructive power of the tongue. We're left to wonder if we should ever speak at all! James doesn't resolve the tension for us. He indicts the tongue, and leaves it before us guilty.

In 3:9, James gives a sort of hint or backhanded acknowledgment of the positive use of the tongue. He writes that with our tongues, we praise God our Father, yet we also curse those who've been made in God's likeness. This divided tongue should not be. But James also shows us one positive use for the tongue: we can use it to praise God. For most of us, words of praise account for a small percentage of our overall speech.

This passage in James features a heavy use of metaphors, and of course, the tongue itself is an analogy. Our tongues don't operate independently of our brains. They don't have their own personality or make their own decisions. Our tongues aren't capable of speaking without our willing them to speak. No, our tongues are merely a dependable barometer of the condition of our hearts. Whatever our minds are full of, our tongues will eventually speak.

Throughout James's letter, we find abundant parallels with Christ's Sermon on the Mount (Matthew 5–7). This suggests that James was either present for Jesus's teaching, or that he had access to later reports of it. Here are some examples of the thematic parallels:

	in Matthew:	in James:
Rejoice and be glad in your trials	5:10-12	1:2
Be perfect and complete	5:48	1:4
Ask your good God who loves you to give you good gifts	7:7-11	1:5,17
Avoid sinful anger	5:22	1:20
Be hearers and not mere doers	7:24-27	1:22
God's heart for the poor in the kingdom	5:3,5	2:5
The necessity of righteousness	5:20	2:10
The merciful will receive mercy	5:7	2:13
Blessed are the peacemakers	7:7-8	3:18
Ask and you will receive	7:7-8	4:2-3
You cannot serve God and be friends with the world	6:4	4:4
Blessed are those who mourn	7:1-5	4:11-12
Be slow to judge	7:1-5	4:11-12
Do not lay up your treasures on earth	6:19	5:2-5

These are only some of the parallels.

James's teaching about the tongue in 3:3-12 is parallel with Matthew 7:15-20—as well as Luke 6:44-45, where Jesus advised his hearers to evaluate a prophet by the quality of his fruit: "For each tree is known by its own fruit. For men do not gather figs from thorns, nor do they pick grapes from a briar bush. The good man out of the good treasure of his heart brings forth what is good; and the evil man out of the evil treasure brings forth what is evil. For his mouth speaks from that which fills his heart."

An apology for something said seems hollow, and forgiveness for a spoken word is difficult to give. This is because speakers generally mean what they say. When a person speaks a cruel or critical word and later says, "I didn't really mean it," we know he's not completely sincere. The speaker meant what he said at some level at least, though he may regret having said it. What hurts is not the words alone, but how they reflect the content of the speaker's heart.

What James is hinting at is that the tongue is indeed untameable, unredeemable, and capable of tremendous evil—unless God redeems the heart for which the tongue speaks.

I don't suggest that we should say everything we think merely because it's an honest reflection of what's in our heart. Even the most spiritually mature among us will have things going through our mind that should remain unspoken. But if our hearts aren't right, we're in constant danger of speaking a destructive word. It's equivalent to walking around while carrying a basket of deadly serpents, inviting an unsuspecting person to lift the lid and suffer a bite.

A tree cannot produce two different kinds of fruit. A stream cannot produce both fresh and salt water. The heart of the Christian should not produce both words glorifying to God and hurtful, destructive words. It's not natural—and yet it frequently occurs.

Trying to bridle our tongue without dealing with the root source in our heart is a bit like fighting an infection by treating the fever. We may temporarily alleviate the symptom, but the infection rages, and the fever will return and worsen until the infection is resolved.

Well, you might ask, what do we do? If James says our efforts to tame our tongue are hopeless, why bother trying? While we may not be able to tame our tongues, we can earnestly seek the transformation of our hearts. When our hearts change, so will our speech. Christians use the word "sanctification" to describe the process of becoming more like Jesus. Sanctification is impossible outside of God's working, and is no less a gift of grace than our salvation (Galatians 3:3). But our role in our sanctification isn't passive. We can actively resist God's working in us, or we can actively yield to it. The Bible is of full of concrete things we can do in cooperation with God in our sanctification:

We can love our friends by laying down our lives for them (John 15).

We can immerse ourselves in God's word so that we're transformed by the renewing of our minds (Romans 12:2).

We husbands can love our wives as much as we love ourselves, by laying down our lives for them (Ephesians 5:25).

Wives can submit to their husbands as to the Lord (Ephesians 5:22).

We can confess our sins to one another and pray for one another, so that our many wounds, including those caused by our tongue, can be healed (James 5:16).

We can give away the possessions that encumber our hearts and distract our minds (1 John 1:15; Luke 18:22).

We can set aside filthiness and wickedness and instead receive God's word, which has been implanted in us (James 1:21).

We can seek to bridle our tongue (James 1:26), because as we pay attention to our speech it will reveal to us the things needing to be confessed or surrendered.

I have one practical tip that may be idiosyncratic to me, but I encourage you to consider it. I've trained myself to pause before answering a question. That sometimes leads to misinterpretation, especially with my wife. She may think I didn't hear her, or I don't know the answer, or I just don't care to respond. Sometimes people will just answer their question themselves before I can start to respond. People can be impatient in conversation, and our culture overvalues rapid speech and quick responses. But I do believe my short pauses have prevented worse consequences. In those few seconds, I can assess the question: What's really being asked? If the person's question concerns something other than a simple fact, I can also assess what consequences are likely to flow from my response. I can also take a quick inventory of my heart to discover what's motivating my response. But practical tips and mere force of will can accomplish little with respect to the untamable tongue. Our tongue will be tamed only when our entire self is submitted to the tamer of all wild things.

Never underestimate the destructive force of the tongue. If James hasn't persuaded you, take an honest look at your own history. In seeking to bridle your own tongue, don't focus on just changing your speech, because speech is primarily a symptom of the condition of your heart. Instead, carefully monitor your speech as you would a fever, allowing it to reveal to you the deeper cause. Only when your heart is transformed is the wild beast tamed.

Discussion Questions

1. Which of the analogies for the tongue in James do you find most challenging or convicting? Why?
2. If someone listened to a recording of your speech over the past week—hearing both the content and the tone—what

would that person likely conclude about the state of your heart?

3. In this chapter we looked at several ways to cooperate with the Lord's transformation of our hearts, as seen in Scripture. In the coming week, what is one way in which you can focus on placing your heart and tongue in submission to God?

17

THE WRONG KIND OF WISDOM

Who among you is wise and understanding?
Let him show by his good behavior his deeds
in the gentleness of wisdom.
But if you have bitter jealousy and selfish ambition
in your heart, do not be arrogant and so lie against the truth.
This wisdom is not that which comes down from above,
but is earthly, natural, demonic. For where jealousy and selfish
ambition exist, there is disorder and every evil thing.

JAMES 3:13-16

I was scrambling to survive. It was very early in my legal career, and I was struggling to pay my office rent and expenses. I was taking any sort of client I could get, and most of what I could get were criminal defense and personal injury clients. I aspired to a career marked with integrity, but I was growing progressively disillusioned with a profession that rewarded hubris and anger. Some lawyers counseled me—either overtly or by example—to be more aggressive, to skirt the ethical edges, and to fight dirty. I looked up to the senior lawyers who drove nice cars and had impressive offices, and a light went on in my head. I wanted what they had, so I determined to mimic their behavior.

In my first case following this epiphany of worldly wisdom, I sent an unreasonably aggressive demand to an insurance company. When I reached the insurance adjuster by phone, I swore, I pounded my desk loud enough that he could hear it on the phone, and I endeavored to cow this man into a favorable settlement. I was really advocating not for my client, but for my one-third contingency fee. I was determined to win big.

James begins this passage by asking, "Who among you is wise and understanding?" I suspect that we all would like to be considered wise, yet there's a scandalous lack of wisdom in our society. Despite our lack of it, wisdom has been a valued trait throughout history and across cultures, even among pagans. Pharaoh consulted wise men when he was confronted with Moses and the plagues (Exodus 7:11). In Esther 1:13, King Ahasuerus consulted his wise men when Queen Vashti rebelled against his command. The pagan king Nebuchadnezzar surrounded himself with the best and brightest men from his broad empire—with Daniel, Shadrach, Meshach, and Abednego among them—and he sought their counsel (Daniel 1:14). Wise men from the east were among the first to recognize the arrival of the Messiah (Matthew 2:1-2). Today our highest-ranking politicians surround themselves with modern versions of wise men and women who are savvy about the acquisition and leverage of power. Yet wise actions out of Washington seem rare. How could something so esteemed, so valuable, and so available be in so little supply? James speaks to that disconnect in this passage.

Wisdom is in short supply because we use the word "wisdom" without appreciating what it really is. We pursue the wrong kind of wisdom and then apply it in the wrong sort of pursuits. James helps us understand what wisdom is by telling us what wisdom is not. Wisdom is shown by gentle good deeds; wisdom is not the skillful controlling of our environment to accomplish selfish pursuits.

If James were presenting this message in person rather than in a letter, I picture him saying, "Who here thinks themselves wise and understanding? Now, if you raised your hand—show me that wisdom by your life." To assume you have wisdom and understanding when the corresponding actions are absent from your life is as hollow as saying you have faith when your life bears no evidence of it.

James knows that his readers think themselves wise, and he's responding, "Baloney!" He has seen them compromise their beliefs in the face of trials. He has witnessed their anger, has heard of their wickedness, and has seen them spout the law while not living by it. He's watched them treat one another with partiality and observed their relentless pursuit of money. He's aware of their adulteries and murders, their lack of mercy, and their untamed and hypocritical speech. James describes all this behavior in his letter. This was the behavior of professed Christians who thought themselves "wise and understanding." James challenges them in this letter, as he now challenges us: If you think you're wise, show me. Show me good behavior, deeds done in the gentleness of wisdom.

Sophos is the Greek adjective James uses in 3:13, and translated as "wise." Noah Webster's 1828 dictionary captures the idea of *sophos* by defining the English word "wisdom" as "the right use or exercise of knowledge; the choice of laudable ends and of the best means to accomplish them.... It is the faculty of discerning or judging what is most just, proper, and useful."[35] Wisdom has also been defined as "insight into the true nature of things."[36] The wisdom of which James writes was not the wisdom of the Greeks, which was an intellectual pursuit cultivated in an academy. The wisdom that James encourages is the ability to see things as God sees them; to view circumstances and people from God's perspective and to act accordingly.

The Greek adjective translated in 3:13 as "understanding" has to do with mental perception; it's closer to our English word "intelligent."[37] The combination of being wise and understanding is both powerful and rare.

The wise person behaves in a way that's good and edifying, a way that builds up and that's above reproach. Such good deeds are done "in the gentleness of wisdom." The *New International Version* translates this as "the humility that comes from wisdom." The truly wise are never haughty in their wisdom, or abusive, or manipulative, or cruel. The wise understand that God is the source of true wisdom; because they know where they stand relative to God, they're humble.

The Greek word translated in 3:13 as "gentleness" means mildness of disposition or gentleness of spirit; it's translated elsewhere in Scripture as "meekness."[38] Most people don't aspire to be meek because they misunderstand the word, thinking it describes weakness or lack of conviction. But this Greek word—*prautes*—describes power manifested in gentleness;[39] it has been likened to a war horse brought under control and trained to take a bridle, imperturbably following commands in the midst of battle. This meekness is strength under control, a useful and purposeful strength directed by a master. A wise person doesn't wield powerful influence to fulfill his own ambitions. A wise person submits to and is directed by God.

The fact that wisdom is shown by gentle good deeds causes

me to ask, "Can we scream wisdom into our children?" (I've tried.) Is it effective to try to impose our "wisdom" on a non-compliant child in a way that isn't gentle? Is the alternative to ungentle behavior either silence or capitulation? This challenges me as a parent, but the image of the yielded horse is useful. I picture tremendous strength under control, a strength so apparent that it need not declare itself, a strength that prompts a healthy fear but also a degree of comfort and protection. The voice of the wise parent is both resolute and gentle, flowing from a confidence in God rather than a fearful effort to gain control.

The word "but" at the beginning of 3:14 is a warning to people who think themselves wise but who fail to exhibit good deeds done in gentleness: "If you have bitter jealousy and selfish ambition in your heart, do not be arrogant and so lie against the truth." In other words, if jealousy is your predominant emotion, and selfish ambition is your ruling motivation—stop lying by saying you have wisdom. Stop being arrogant by claiming to be something you're not. Arrogant people think they have wisdom because their idea of wisdom is false. That wisdom is not from above—it's not of God. Such wisdom is earthly, natural, and demonic.

The wisdom to which James calls us isn't the kind of practical wisdom that answers the question, "Should I sell all my Apple stock, or has it already bottomed out?" If that's how it worked, Christian stockbrokers would rule the world. This is the great mistake we often make in seeking wisdom from God; we think of it as special knowledge from God that allows us to increase our comfort. But wisdom from God conforms us to the image of Christ and has nothing to do with obtaining the objects of our jealousy or selfish ambitions.

In the work world, we observe how skills of deceit, manipulation, and intimidation often seem to win the day. Because this "wisdom" has apparent benefit, we may be tempted to imitate it. Such conduct springs from jealousy and selfish ambition, not godly wisdom. Many business books teach the wrong type of wisdom, yet we Christians gobble them up and exhibit conduct in the workplace that's indistinguishable from the behavior of any pagan. That "wisdom" is earthly, natural, and even demonic. The wrong kind of wisdom may appear to bear fruit, but it's not a good harvest. The fruit is disorder and every evil thing.

Worldly wisdom manipulates, intimidates, deceives, and exerts power in an effort to obtain materialistic or ego-driven aims. The wrong sort of wisdom produces a disordered life full of misplaced priorities, broken relationships, money that goes as easily as it comes, substance abuse to anesthetize the consequent pain, and disciples who imitate that behavior and duplicate that fruit. Earthly wisdom is excellent at convincing us that we're doing better than we really are, parting a fool from his money, evading the law, seducing a woman, or cowing a subordinate into frightened submission. These are evil fruits born from the wrong kind of wisdom.

James calls us to godly wisdom evidenced by a well-ordered life under God, a life characterized by goodness and humility.

Now, back to my office many years ago, when I was pounding my desk and swearing into the phone. The insurance adjuster, an older man, was aghast; he chastised me for my arrogant and abusive behavior. I was embarrassed. My effort at winning by intimidation was comically ineffective. I came off like a kid wearing someone else's ill-fitting suit. It did not become me. I retreated and returned another day, armed with preparation rather than attitude, motivated by advocacy for my client rather than selfish ambition. I negotiated a fair settlement, and stored the memory.

For twenty years now, I've been a transactional lawyer, primarily in real estate. In negotiating contracts, structuring joint ventures, and closing deals, it can still seem that hubris and anger win the day, so I'm still tempted at times to adopt worldly wisdom. To employ godly wisdom requires faith in the God who gives it, because it runs counter to the strident voices of worldly wisdom. If I want to walk in godly wisdom, I must marinate in the truths of God's word. Otherwise, the siren call of earthly wisdom will lure me to the rocks.

Do you think yourself wise and understanding? Then examine your life and take an honest inventory. Do you evidence good deeds done in gentleness, or evil disorder? Most of us, I suspect, display some of both. Let's use such a personal inventory to identify where we're applying false wisdom, and to repent. Let's invite God to redeem those unsurrendered corners by filling us with his true wisdom.

Discussion Questions

1. Before you read this chapter, if you'd been asked to define or describe a wise person, what might you have come up with?
2. Why do you think bitter jealousy and selfish ambitions can be litmus tests of not having wisdom? How might having a heart of wisdom prevent bitter jealousy and selfish ambitions from reigning in our hearts?
3. We've seen that wisdom from God allows us to see circumstances and people from God's perspective, and to act accordingly. Can you think of a time in your life when you

began to view circumstances and people from God's per-spective? How did he develop that in you? What was the effect?

4. In your life's daily environments, what struggles do you face in attempting to live by God's view of wisdom, instead of the world's?

18

THE RIGHT KIND
OF WISDOM

But the wisdom from above is first pure, then peaceable,
gentle, reasonable, full of mercy and good fruits, unwavering,
without hypocrisy. And the seed whose fruit is righteousness
is sown in peace by those who make peace.

JAMES 3:17-18

As I write this chapter, my wife and I are trying to make wise decisions with respect to our house. Our house is functional but somewhat worn, after fourteen years of hosting our rambunctious family of six. Holes, scuffs, and elementary school art projects adorn our walls. The carpet is older than our oldest child (who's now in college), and much of our furniture consists of pressboard in a state of partial collapse. Our house is not, by suburban Atlanta standards, impressive. Besides considering whether to replace the carpet, we've looked also at repaving the driveway or updating the bathrooms and basement. When we resolve to do any one particular thing, it seems to lead to a dozen other related things, and it all carries a significant price tag. We pray about these decisions daily. But God doesn't speak to us in an audible voice, saying, "Pave the driveway, but hold off on the bathrooms." He could, but that's not how he typically deals with his people. I suspect that many who claim to receive that sort of specific direction from God are failing to discern between the voices in their own head and divine direction.

Does godly wisdom play a role in these sorts of practical decisions? If so, how do Christians make wise decision with respect to something like a house renovation?

Godly wisdom is identifiable by its characteristics and by its fruit. In the previous verses, James described the wrong sort of wisdom, an earthly wisdom characterized by envy and selfish ambition and bearing the fruit of disorder and every evil thing. The wrong sort of wisdom predominates in our culture, as evidenced by our relentless pursuit of material possessions, status, and physical beauty. These vain pursuits produce anger, high divorce rates, and an increasingly disconnected and discontented society. The reverse image of that is what characterizes godly wisdom: gentleness and reasonableness, and a harvest of righteousness and peace.

James says that wisdom is first of all pure. Purity, rather than intelligence, is wisdom's chief characteristic. To be pure is to be chaste and free from defilement or impurities.[40] If we have a thought or opinion we think is wise, but which is tainted by impurity, then it isn't wisdom. It may be a popular opinion, well received, articulately presented, and even effective in achieving certain results, but if it isn't pure, it's not wisdom. False wisdom often flows from selfish desires, lust, or revenge. Godly wisdom is free of these things; it is first pure.

Godly wisdom, James says, is also peaceable. Are there purportedly wise people in your life who stir up anger and fighting whenever they speak? Then you must question whether they have wisdom at all. The Christian church needs its prophets, those people of strong conviction who call the people of God to repentance. But Christians with a prophetic temperament sometimes lack wisdom in their presentation of truth. Without wisdom, truth can become a bludgeon that produces bitterness rather than repentance. In this era of social media, many Christians subject their followers to a constant stream of pugnacious messages and articles designed to agitate rather than bring the peace of godly reconciliation. This isn't wisdom; it isn't godly, and it produces no good fruit.

Wisdom is gentle. The Greek term translated here as "gentle" includes the notions of moderation and patience.[41] False wisdom is often harsh, cruel, demanding, and demeaning. Godly wisdom is gentle, nurturing, and mindful of the heart.

James says that wisdom is both "reasonable" as well as "unwavering." These characteristics would seem to be in conflict, because to be reasonable is to be persuadable by argument,[42] whereas to be unwavering is to be unyielding. However, these traits coexist in a truly wise person. A wise person is yielding with respect to nonessentials, and amenable to persuasion in matters that aren't specifically addressed by clear biblical mandates. However, with respect to theological essentials and the clear mandates of God, the wise person is unyielding. An unwise person cannot distinguish between the areas in which they're to be open to change and where they should be unwavering. The wise man recognizes where he may yield, and where he must make his stand without compromise.

Wisdom is merciful. Wisdom doesn't delight in punishment, but in repentance. Wisdom doesn't seek opportunities for revenge or rejoice in negative consequences for wrongs. Instead, wisdom is merciful as our heavenly Father is merciful. One Greek dictionary defines mercy as "a special and immediate regard to the misery which is the consequence of sins."[43] Wisdom's mercy is more than withholding punishment; it extends compassionate help to those who are suffering from the consequences of their sin. God's first inclination toward his people is mercy. Throughout the Old Testament, God pursued his people primarily with mercy—it came in countless forms, including an ark, covenants, a sacrificial system, judges, prophets, and a prophesied Messiah. Punishment came when God's people persisted in rejecting his mercy. Still today, God reserves vengeance to himself; it's never ours to implement (Romans 12:19-21). Wisdom brings the merciful character of our Father into broken situations brought about by bad decisions and sinful conduct. Wisdom acts toward broken sinners with grace, with practical assistance, and with truth.

Wisdom is full of good fruits. It produces good things. If the products of a person's life are primarily anger, malice, selfishness, greed, and broken relationships, such a person is not wise. A life conducted with wisdom produces love, joy, peace, patience, kindness, goodness, faithfulness, gentleness and self-control (Galatians 5:22-23).

Wisdom is without hypocrisy. To be a hypocrite is to pretend or simulate.[44] Some people are more concerned with appearing to be wise than actually seeking wisdom. Such people often appear wise in public, and yet have a family life or personal life full of envy, strife, selfish ambition, and disorder. True wisdom is evidenced within the walls of a person's home as well as in the church pew.

In 3:18, James amplifies the importance of peace in a wise person's life, and he links peace with righteousness. If we want to encourage righteousness in others—whether children, employees, students, or disciples—we must be people who make peace. This is a challenge to me as a parent, because my kids sometimes do sinful or thoughtless things which anger me. But anger masquerading as wisdom produces rebellion, whereas seeds sown in peace produce righteousness. Inherent in this verse and in James's overall discussion on wisdom is that wisdom requires trust in a mighty and righteous God to bring about his ultimate ends, including in our children. Earthly wisdom values self-determination. Godly wisdom cultivates dependence on God. The wise person has surrendered the illusion of control.

Too often, we limit the concept of wisdom by thinking of it as a specific direction with respect to a particular decision. We want God to tell us whether to take a particular job, or to marry a particular person, or to buy a particular car. Though godly wisdom is useful in making these sorts of decisions, such wisdom rarely comes in the form of a specific dictate from above. God doesn't send emails. This is because God's primary concern is not what job we take, what person we marry, or what car we buy. Those particulars consume our attention and emotion, but God's primary concern, as evidenced in the many stories he provides us in his word, is with the development of our godly character.

My wife and I need to make decisions about our house. We want to make wise decisions, but God doesn't text us or speak from the sky in an audible voice to tell us whether we should renovate. If we rely on the voices in our heads, the noise of our own desires will drown out the still small voice of God. Many Christians pray about a decision, then sanctify their natural desires by saying, "I prayed about it." Going by gut is an extremely unreliable and generally self-serving way to discern the will of God.

How then does a Christian go about making a decision on a matter that isn't related to any clear biblical mandate? I recommend that we consider the characteristics of wisdom James has given us. For my wife and me, our decision-making goes something like this: Wisdom is first pure, so I have to ask why I'm pursuing this. Why do I want to renovate our house? Is it because I want our place to give people the impression that I'm successful? If so, my motive is impure and thus unwise. Or am I desiring to serve my family and create a place where we can more effectively host and minister?

Wisdom is peaceable. If we opt to refurbish the house, will we introduce unwanted conflict and stress into our marriage? Are we unified in our decision, or am I imposing my will on my wife without her confirming voice?

Wisdom is reasonable. Have I taken an honest look at our budget to determine whether we can responsibly take this step, or am I presuming on God to provide as I voluntarily over-extend our finances?

Wisdom is without hypocrisy. Would I give someone else the same advice I'm giving myself in this situation? Do I hold others to different standards than I hold myself? Am I pretending to have a pure motive when in fact envy and selfish ambition fuel my motives? As I solicit an opinion from a Christian brother, am I withholding bits of information to shape his opinion and make myself look more spiritual than I really am?

This kind of thorough self-assessment should govern all our decisions. Scripture doesn't tell me specifically whether I should renovate my house; it does tell me to walk in wisdom, and it tells me what wisdom looks like. God is far less concerned with the appearance of my house than he is with the development of my character. Consequently, he might want me to renovate my house knowing that the process will be full of struggles, stresses, and difficulties, which he'll use to cultivate my humility and to prepare me to advise others in similar situations. We should never assume that every wise decision will lead to ease, while only poor decisions lead to difficulty. The most godly of decisions may lead to suffering, because through such experiences we grow in Christ. Without suffering, we remain spiritual infants.

Godly wisdom doesn't necessarily result in earthly gain, but it always results in godly fruit. We're citizens of God's kingdom, and strangers and aliens on this earth. Therefore, as we walk in this foreign land, we must walk in godly wisdom rather than the wisdom of this world. The fruit of godly wisdom is righteousness, mercy, and peace.

Discussion Questions

1. In this chapter, what for you was most challenging or most compelling?
2. The list of characteristics of wisdom from 3:17 are similar to the description Paul gives for the fruit of the Spirit (read Galatians 5:22-23). Is this similarity purely coincidental, or do you think there are connections we can draw?
3. How does one go about developing these traits of wisdom in James 3:17, especially as compared to how one would seek to develop the fruit of the Spirit?
4. James 3:18 states, "And the seed whose fruit is righteousness is sown in peace by those who make peace." In what ways do you think this statement links with the listed characteristics of wisdom in 3:17?
5. What might "sowing in peace" look like?

19

THE SOURCE OF CONFLICT

What is the source of quarrels and conflicts among you?
Is not the source your pleasures that wage war in your members?
You lust and do not have; so you commit murder.
You are envious and cannot obtain; so you fight and quarrel.
You do not have because you do not ask. You ask and
do not receive, because you ask with wrong motives,
so that you may spend it on your pleasures.

JAMES 4:1-3

When my children were young, I marveled at their propensity to quarrel. It's instructive to observe young children because they exhibit unvarnished human nature. Sister would have a toy that brother wanted, so brother would force it from her. Brother would have something sister wanted, so she would cry and manipulate a grownup to get it for her. Little sister would get positive attention for something, and big sister would throw a fit to get attention herself. Little brother would fly into a rage over a profound injustice like getting the smaller bowl of ice cream or finding the cereal box empty because another sibling beat him to breakfast. Man's sinful nature is on full display in a house with four children.

Are we adults so different? We've learned that overt jealousy and selfish ambition are not attractive traits, so we're more subtle than small children are. At core, however, jealousy and selfish ambition sometimes still rule our hearts. If you doubt this, watch adult children dividing an inheritance. Or sit in a workplace breakroom after the annual compensation memos have been distributed. Or sit in Atlanta traffic during rush hour and watch the aggressive behavior of thousands racing to save a few minutes on their way to work. Or sit on the sidelines of a youth soccer match when the referee awards the other team a dubious penalty. In those settings, the latent toddler in us comes out—and we fight. We fight for what we think we should possess, or for the status we think we should have, or for our perceived sense of fairness toward ourselves.

The Bible's King Ahab (in 1 Kings 21) is an example of this sort of behavior. The king had a neighbor named Naboth who owned a beautiful vineyard next to the king's palace. The king wanted to buy the vineyard and turn it into a vegetable garden. Naboth didn't want to sell because it was his inheritance and he wanted to keep it for his descendants. Ahab countered, "But I'll give you another piece of property, or I'll pay you a good price for it." Naboth still refused, so King Ahab went home and pouted. The Bible says he was "sullen and vexed." He laid down, turned his face toward the wall, and wouldn't eat. His inner toddler came out.

Ahab's not so lovely wife, Jezebel, was disgusted by her husband's pouting. "You're the king of Israel!" she said. "Get up! I'll get you the vineyard." She arranged to have some ne'er-do-wells falsely accuse Naboth of heresy, and the elders of the city stoned Naboth to death. Ahab got his vineyard, but Ahab and his wife were forever cursed.

Murder is extreme, but it's the logical outcome when people are unrestrained in their pursuit of pleasure. In James 4:1, the Greek words translated as "quarrels" and "conflicts" literally mean "battles" and "wars."[45] These words reference both smaller squabbles between individuals and broader conflicts among groups of people.

The source of these conflicts, James says, is our pleasures. The word translated as "pleasures" in 4:3 refers to our sensual delight.[46] There's nothing wrong with sensual delight. God gave us noses to smell bread baking in the oven, eyes to watch the sun set over the ocean, fingers to caress the soft face of an infant, ears to hear majestic sounds of a well-trained choir, and tongues to taste our favorite meals. God created human bodies wired for pleasure, and he made our world in which sensual delights abound. In fact, some of the most delightful passages in Scripture call upon our senses to celebrate the character of God: "Taste and see that the Lord is good" (Psalm 34:8); "You will make known to me the path of life; in your presence is the fullness of joy; in your right hand there are pleasures forever" (Psalm 16:11). The Song of Solomon is both allegorical and a celebration of the sexual pleasure to be enjoyed between husband and wife.

However, Scripture also warns us against allowing our pursuit of pleasure to rule over us. The sin of sensuality is an overindulgence in the senses without restraint or discrimination. It's a life devoted to the pursuit of pleasure.

Now the deeds of the flesh are evident, which are: immorality, impurity, sensuality, idolatry, sorcery, enmities, strife, jealousy, outbursts of anger, disputes, dissensions, factions, envying, drunkenness, carousing, and things like these, of which I forewarn you, just as I have forewarned you, that those who practice such things will not inherit the kingdom of God. (Galatians 5:19-21)

Paul accuses some of worshiping their stomach as a god (Philippians 3:18-19). Peter reminds us that slavery to sensual pleasure should be a thing of the past for the Christian, "For the time already past is sufficient for you to have carried out the desire of the Gentiles, having pursued a course of sensuality, lusts, drunkenness, carousing, drinking parties and abominable idolatries" (1 Peter 4:3). We fall short of what God intends when we allow a good thing, such as a sensual delight, to become an ultimate thing.

Obtaining pleasure is the primary motivation of this world. In fact, from a secular viewpoint, the aim of life is to maximize pleasure and minimize pain. But earthly pleasures are fleeting. If we make pleasure our god, we live with perpetual discontentment. Unless we're vigilant, Christians can also fall prey to being consumed with pleasure seeking.

When pleasure becomes our god, yet we don't receive all the pleasures we desire (and we never do), we become angry, jealous, and resentful. So we fight. This is true of individuals, of families, communities, and nations. We don't get the pleasures we want, or fear the loss of the pleasures we have, and we resort to violent conflict in an effort to secure more pleasure.

James says that we want things we don't have, so we commit murder. Not many of us are guilty of literal murder, but how often have we killed in our heart through hatred or with our tongue through slander? Christ says in the Sermon on the Mount that when we hate someone, we have in essence murdered that person (Matthew 5:21-22). Our hatred often stems from our belief that someone has taken something that rightfully belongs to us—whether a possession, political power, a relationship, an experience, or recognition. When someone takes what we think should be ours, we often slay that person in our hearts. How many of us have nursed a grudge for years because someone didn't reciprocate our affection, didn't pay us what was owed, or took more than their fair share? How many of us have killed someone's reputation with our slander because we're angry or envious? When envy turns into actions and words, it looks a lot like war.

James says an interesting thing in 4:2."You do not have, because you do not ask." We can and should ask God for things. James isn't the only authority in the Bible who says this. Jesus told us to ask, and it would be given to us (Matthew 7:7). Paul tells us to bring all our requests before God (Philippians 4:6). James's readers failed to ask God for what they needed. We often exclude God from the practical spheres of our lives, and we sin when we fail to bring our whole selves under his authority. The act of asking is inherently submissive, and so we sometimes resent it. When it comes to our relationship with God, there's no room for rugged individualism. We need to ask. The act of asking increases our dependence on God.

We don't always get the things we ask for, and James gives a partial explanation for those unfulfilled requests in 4:3. He says that we don't get what we ask for because we ask with the motive of spending what we get on our pleasures. If you strip away the veneer of our requests to God, many of our prayers are disguised pleas for more money. It's not necessarily wrong to pray for money, because we all need it. But we must guard our hearts against greed. Are you asking for more money because you have a legitimate need or because you have a strong desire for pleasure? Are you asking to have enough money so you don't have to depend on God? It's a mercy when God doesn't give us the idols for which we ask him.

Some false teachers have ripped Scripture out of its context and used it to support a prosperity gospel.[47] This false gospel teaches that God's primary aim for us is that we experience this world's pleasures. The prosperity gospel presents a formula: we need only ask in faith for what we want, and God will give it to us. According to these false teachers, if we don't get what we ask for, it's because we don't have enough faith. The prosperity gospel converts doctrine into magic and Scripture into an incantation. It elevates our desires above God's will. God's chief aim for us is not to maximize our pleasure, but to help us become like him: "Be perfect, even as your heavenly Father is perfect" (Matthew 5:48); "Those God foreknew, he predestined to become conformed to the image of his Son" (Romans 8:29).

God isn't a power we can manipulate to get what we want, like Santa Claus or a genie. God is our Father. Like all good fathers, he gives good gifts, and every good gift is from him (James 1:17). We don't always get what we want, but that doesn't mean our heavenly Father isn't good. Good fathers don't overindulge or give gifts that aren't in their children's best interest.

When our eldest was a toddler, he saw a big shiny something on the kitchen counter that he desperately wanted to play with. He used all his limited communication skills to entreat us, and he did so with confidence. That something he wanted was a sharp kitchen knife. Instead of giving our toddler a knife, we said "No" and moved it out of reach. He reacted as though we'd stabbed him with it. He threw himself on the floor, screamed, and thrashed. His tantrum went on for a long time, but we weren't going to give him that knife.

Sometimes God, the giver of all good gifts, refuses to hand us the kitchen knife. With our limited perspective, we're as unable to discern between what's good and what isn't as two-year-old Jack was unable to discern the danger of the kitchen knife. When pleasure rules our existence and we measure the quality of our life by sensual delight, we can easily grow disillusioned with God when our pleasures are lacking. But when we begin to define the quality of our life as God defines it (which is another way to describe wisdom), we begin to see God's greater plan at work.

I don't mean to trivialize the pain of unanswered prayer. Sometimes we ask for things that seem unequivocally good and in accordance with God's will, but we don't get them. Perhaps we pray for physical healing or the salvation of someone we love, but instead we suffer loss. The prosperity gospel puts the blame on the asker who didn't ask with enough faith, but that's a false and heavy yoke. God is in control, no matter the strength of our belief. There are no easy answers in these situations, but we must accept in faith that we have a very limited perspective. We don't have the capacity to know the intricate workings of a sovereign God. It's only with hindsight that we begin to understand God's aims, and that hindsight may not be available until we see him face to face (1 Corinthians 13:12).

When we're walking with and abiding in God, our prayers take on a different character. We spend less time asking for the things to satisfy our sensual appetites, and we start praying for truly significant things. We begin to imitate Christ, who in his high priestly prayer asked for unity among his disciples, for love, and for godly joy (John 17:1-26). We begin to pray like Paul who prayed for spiritual growth, patience, comprehension, knowledge, and other enduring and godly traits (Ephesians 1:17-19; 3:16-19; Philippians 1:9-11; Colossians 1:9-12). When we pray like this, we experience more answers to our prayer because we're praying in cooperation with God, consistent with his aims for us and with his character. When we begin to see as God sees, our greatest delights are not fleeting sensual pleasures, but the enduring things of the kingdom of God. These eternal ambitions never lead to competition and envy, because they don't diminish when we share them with others; instead they grow.

It's not wrong to take delight in sensual pleasure, but we sin when we become enslaved to the pursuit of pleasure. When our appetite is our god, we'll succumb to envy and hatred. James urges us to seek God as the source of good gifts, and he entreats us to search our hearts for false motives. Though we resist it, there's far greater joy in the life submitted to God than in the life devoted to pleasure. The submitted life is "that which is life indeed" (1 Timothy 6:19).

Discussion Questions

1. James summarizes the source of conflicts and quarrels among these first-century Jewish Christians as their pursuit of pleasure and the satisfaction of their desires. Would you say this is any different for twenty-first-century Christians? How so?

2. What are some explanations people sometimes give for why God doesn't always answer prayer? How do these compare with what James is saying in 4:3?

3. As you review the following passages from earlier in James—1:14-15; 2:3-4; 3:9-11; and 3:16-17—what common themes do you see?

4. How do we go about recalibrating the true motivations of our hearts, so that we pray with right motives? Can you think of a time or season in your life when you experienced a recalibration of the motives of your own heart? What did that look like?

20

WHO DO
YOU LOVE?

You adulteresses, do you not know
that friendship with the world is hostility toward God?
Therefore whoever wishes to be a friend of the world makes
himself an enemy of God. Or do you think that the Scripture
speaks to no purpose: "He jealously desires the Spirit which
he has made to dwell in us"? But he gives a greater grace.
Therefore it says, "God is opposed to the proud,
but gives grace to the humble."

James 4:4-6

In 1957, Bo Diddley asked the musical question, "Who do you love?" You might have asked someone the same question in the past. Some have had to ask it during seasons of marriage when hearts have wandered or grown cold.

Who do you love? This is the core question James is asking in 4:4-6. Do you love the Lord Jesus Christ, or do you love the world? Christians know the "right" answer, but what answer truly reflects the state of our hearts? Scripture's greatest command is "You shall love the Lord your God with all your heart, and with

140

all your soul, and with all your mind and with all your strength" (Matthew 22:36-40). Yet our hearts are easily seduced by other loves (Mark 12:30). In this passage, James identifies our all-too-frequent mistress while calling us to a greater love. He also writes that God's grace covers even our lack of love, because we all fall short of this greatest command.

New Testament writers refer to Christ as the bridegroom and the church as his bride (Ephesians 5:25-27; 2 Corinthians 11:2). The church is betrothed to Christ (2 Corinthians 11:2). The Hebrew concept of betrothal was like our concept of engagement, but more binding. Mary was betrothed to Joseph at the time of Christ's birth. They hadn't yet consummated their marriage, but a divorce would have been required to break their betrothal (Matthew 1:19). The Jewish betrothal period was designed to allow the bridegroom to first pay the bride price and then prepare a house for his bride. Afterward, he would take a loud procession to his bride's house for the wedding feast.[48] This was part of the cultural background when Jesus said to his disciples, "I go to prepare a place for you. If I go and prepare a place for you, I will come again and receive you to Myself, that where I am, there you may be also" (John 14:2-3). In Revelation 19, the apostle John hears a heavenly throng announcing a wedding that occurs when Christ's work is complete, and God's kingdom is finally triumphant. The betrothal of the church will become a marriage at the great wedding feast, and John hears an angel describing it as "the marriage supper of the lamb" (Revelation 19:7-8).

God loves his people, his church, with a passionate and righteous possessiveness. All too often, what we return to him is adultery. This imagery of God as husband and his people as unfaithful wife is repeated throughout Scripture. The Old

Testament contains vivid descriptions of the adulterous behavior of God's chosen people. In Ezekiel 23, the Lord tells his prophet an allegory of the sisters Oholah and Oholibah, who represent God's people, who were unfaithful brides, often looking to other men to satisfy both their needs and their pleasures. God says this about Oholibah (symbolizing Jerusalem):

> Yet she multiplied her harlotries, remembering the days of her youth, when she played the harlot in the land of Egypt. She lusted after their paramours, whose flesh is like the flesh of donkeys and whose issue is like the issue of horses. Thus you longed for the lewdness of your youth, when the Egyptians handled your bosom because of the breasts of your youth. (Ezekiel 23:19-21)

If this imagery makes you uncomfortable, it should. Adultery in the face of perfect love is disturbing and offensive. When a man tenderly loves and provides for his bride, he's right to expect her faithfulness in return. Note the disparity of obligations in the relationship between God and his people. One sacrificially protects, provides, and nurtures; the role of the other is simply to be faithful and to never look elsewhere for that care, support, and provision. We commit adultery when we look to this world to satisfy our desires instead of looking to God.

Some will point out an apparent contradiction in Scripture. John 3:16 and other passages tell us that God loves the world. Should we not also love the world as he does? But God's loving the world involves his love of the people in it. James's warning against loving the world involves the systems, values, and secular order of this world. The same man who wrote John 3:16 also wrote 1 John 2:15-17, which says:

Do not love the world nor the things in the world. If anyone loves the world, the love of the Father is not in him. For all that is in the world, the lust of the flesh and the lust of the eyes and the boastful pride of life, is not from the Father, but is from the world. The world is passing away, and also its lusts; but the one who does the will of God lives forever.

Jesus said that the second greatest commandment is this: "You shall love your neighbor as yourself." We're to love the people in this world, but we're not to love the systems and values of this world—the lust of the flesh, the lust of the eyes, and the boastful pride of life. We must learn to love the people in this earth without assimilating in a foreign culture that rejects God.

James accuses his readers of being adulteresses because of their *phileo* with the world—their commonality of interests. This challenges me, because I also have a commonality of interests with the world. Too often, the things necessary for life on this earth—working and earning to have shelter and food—can become what my life is about. I look to the systems of this earth to provide for my needs. I derive too much significance from attaining a status the world considers worthy. I long to be attractive in my appearance and in my bearing in the eyes of the world rather than the eyes of God. I subscribe to the great fallacy of the modern church—the both/and. I want to call myself a passionate, single-minded follower of Christ, but I also want a life that's enviable by earthly standards. In God's economy, however, whoever wants to save his life must lose it (Matthew 16:25).

The Bible is full of stories of faithful people who faced similar temptations. Esther was in exile from her native country, a stranger in a strange land. The Persian king chose Esther as his queen because of her great beauty. This young exile suddenly attained high status in the greatest empire the world had ever known. Then she learned that the king's second-in-command planned to kill her fellow Jews. She faced a choice: Would she preserve her position, becoming a friend of this world? Or would she risk it all to serve the people of God? Rather than luxuriating in her role as queen, she recognized that she'd attained her elevated status for a greater purpose than personal comfort. She'd been elevated to that status not to serve herself, but to serve the people of God. She risked not only her status but her life, and in doing so she honored God and saved her people from massacre.

A little before Esther on the historical timeline, Daniel, Shadrach, Meshach, and Abed-nego were also exiles. Their Babylonian captors recognized the brilliance and talent of these young men and gave them privileged positions in an academy designed to train advisers for the king. These young exiles could have chosen the path of selfish enjoyment, eating extravagant foods, and embracing their newfound status. Instead, they risked both their position and their lives by choosing to honor God rather than their earthly king.

All these people managed to attain comfort in a place of exile, where they were strangers and aliens. They risked loss of that comfort to serve the greater kingdom of which they were true citizens.

What are we choosing today? Are we imitating these great saints of old by choosing our God as our highest allegiance? Or are we seeking to become comfortable, high-ranking citizens of the kingdom where we live in exile? It's getting less and less comfortable here for the people of God. That's both a challenge and a blessing. The challenges are obvious. The blessing is that it's becoming harder to live the both/and lie that promotes our wholehearted allegiance to both the eternal and the earthly.

The seductions of this world are often subtle. A little success and a flattering whisper in the ear seduces us to a source of satisfaction other than our Bridegroom. We want to be friendly with the world. We gauge the effectiveness of our faith by how much the world likes us. We live to please this world, despite Jesus's promise that the world would hate us because it hated him (John 15:18).

Political power is one of the great seductions for American Christians. Christians should be active in our political process, but we err when we place our hope in it. God doesn't need political power to achieve his ends. We place too much hope in a system of the world to give us peace and provision. Like a bride, we should have only one source for these things. When we look elsewhere, we commit spiritual adultery.

God is jealous for our affections. He has placed his Spirit in those of us who believe in him, and he jealousy longs for the unity that comes from our faithful, wholehearted allegiance to him.

Yet none of us loves God perfectly. To varying degrees, we all succumb to the temptation of being a friend with this world. This is why James says of God, "But he gives a greater grace." God's grace is sufficient to cover our lack of faithfulness, and he still loves his bride despite her adultery.

God gives us the story of Hosea to demonstrate his persistent love for us. Hosea took a prostitute as his wife, knowing she would be unfaithful. She was unfaithful, but Hosea took her in and loved her, then took her back and loved her again. In the same way, God loves us and won't stop loving us.

James concludes this passage with an admonition that we should come before God humbly. When we do, and we confess our adultery rather than brashly demanding a greater friendship with the world in the form of greater status and comfort, we find ourselves in cooperation with God rather than in opposition to him. He gives greater grace.

God isn't keeping us from good things. The seductions of this earth never deliver what they promise, but only distract us and keep us from true joy and peace.

The most fulfilling earthly relationship comes from a lifetime commitment to one person, forsaking all others. The most fulfilling spiritual relationship comes from a similar monogamy. The apostle John tells us that our heavenly Father has lavished a great love on us (1 John 3:1). This is God's aim for his beloved: to lavish love on us. He asks that we not stray from his love. His desire for our faithfulness stems not from his need for our faithfulness, but from his earnest desire that his children experience the fullness of his love.

Discussion Questions

1. Think back to times in your life when you were most fulfilled. What were the reasons for this fulfillment?

2. We often seek security outside of the Lord without even realizing it. Once we sense that something's amiss, it's easy to treat the symptom rather than the root cause. How can we go about ensuring that our love is completely for the Lord?

3. We've seen how temptation in this world is often very subtle. It can creep into our lives even when we're trying to

show Christ's love to nonbelievers around us. Practically, how can we remain vigilant and jealously guard our love for the Lord?

4. Immediately after talking about the adulterous heart, James mentions pride and humility. What connection do you see between these concepts in your own life?

21

SPIRITUAL WARFARE

Submit therefore to God. Resist the devil
and he will flee from you. Draw near to God
and he will draw near to you. Cleanse your hands,
you sinners; and purify your hearts, you double-minded.
Be miserable and mourn and weep; let your laughter
be turned into mourning and your joy to gloom.
Humble yourselves in the presence of the Lord,
and he will exalt you.

JAMES 4:7-10

In the summer of 1988, I served with a team of missionaries in a Thai jungle near the Laotian border. A brief border war between the countries had ended in February, but one sweltering day we heard distant artillery, initially mistaking it for thunder. Scores of military helicopters zoomed overhead toward the apparent conflict. We thought about leaving, but the locals didn't seem terribly alarmed, so we stayed. To this day, I don't know what was happening, but that physical battle foreshadowed the spiritual battle to come.

That evening, we trekked deeper into the jungle to show *The Jesus Film* to an isolated people group. We connected the

148

projector to a generator and tied a sheet to some trees as a makeshift screen. The curious townspeople gathered and squatted. Old and young alike improbably folded themselves with their feet flat on the ground, their posterior hovering inches above the dirt, and their hands and chins resting on their knees. As the sun descended, we heard a cacophony of drums and aggressive chants emanating from the jungle nearby. Through interpreters, we learned that a group of animists was opposing our visit, calling on spirits to interrupt the showing.

The movie started without trouble. Dubbed in the Thai language, it told the story of Jesus from the Gospel of John. The villagers were entranced with the novelty of the film, but the eerie sound of the animist ceremony created unease. As the cacophony reached a crescendo, the wind kicked up, and a corner of our makeshift screen came loose and flapped. The projector began to chatter and the projected image vibrated. The external speaker inexplicably fell from its perch. The villagers became visibly disturbed, and some left. One of our team members became violently ill. The projector bulb popped and went dark. Finally, the projector seized altogether. All the while, the chants and drums echoed. I've never sensed a more palpable malevolent presence than I felt at that moment. One of the older women with our team, a Filipina, seemed unsurprised. She simply said, "I sense opposition. I think we should pray."

Our team gathered and prayed. A couple of people took the sick team member to a larger village with a doctor. The rest of us tied down the screen, returned the speaker to its perch, and started up the generator again. I was skeptical because I'd never seen a blown bulb regenerate, and we had no extras. To my surprise, the projector started up, the bulb projected the image onto the screen, and we completed the film without further incident.

When it was over, we used the interpreters to invite anyone who wanted to talk more about Jesus to join us at our compound several miles away. The villagers' collective expression was inscrutable. I was relieved to leave that place, and had little expectation that our visit had borne any fruit.

We were staying a few miles away in the house of a local Christian family, little more than a roof and floor. After a fitful sleep in the buggy, humid jungle, the father of the house woke us with excited shouts. More than a dozen young men from the community where we had shown the film were waiting for us to wake so they could learn more about Jesus. The God we represented had won the prior night's conflict, and they wanted to learn more about him.

I hesitate to share that story, because the modern mind is skeptical. Many readers will discredit the story, attributing it to a lack of veracity, the hyperbole of distant memory, or natural explanations. But I know what happened, because it happened to me. I was engaged in spiritual warfare.

Ever since that night, I've looked back on that experience as a reminder that "our struggle is not against flesh and blood, but against the rulers, against the powers, against the world forces of this darkness, against the spiritual forces of wickedness in the heavenly places" (Ephesians 6:12).

The notion of spiritual warfare can seem exotic and strange, and even embarrassing to "sophisticated" Christians. But Jesus engaged in spiritual warfare throughout his earthly ministry. Jesus either had direct and literal conflicts with Satan and his demons, or we must dismiss the gospels as myth.

The conflict continues in the church age. There was no allegory in Paul's statement about our fight against the spiritual forces of wickedness. Many missionaries serving in the remote parts of the world can tell stories similar to the one I related here. But most of us haven't experienced anything like it—not because our enemy is inactive, but because he's clever. The cultivation of unbelief is his most effective weapon in our western culture, so overt supernatural displays are not an effective tactic. Depression, anxiety, unbelief, the seduction of riches and comfort—these are the salvos of spiritual warfare in the western world. But we don't recognize the enemy's schemes, or even acknowledge that we're at war, so we lose for lack of fighting.

We're all at war, whether we would choose it or not. Our adversaries include the world, the flesh, and the devil (Ephesians 2:23). Some shrink from the fight while others deny its existence. Still others picture themselves the hero of the story, bravely wielding a sword against a doomed foe. James condemns both approaches here, calling the doves to action and the hawks to humility.

In his first epistle, the apostle John instructs us not to love the world or anything in the world because such love is incompatible with the love of the Father in us (1 John 2:15). Yet the world constantly tempts us with fleeting pleasures, false peace, and counterfeit righteousness. Paul points out that our flesh is in opposition to the Holy Spirit within us (Galatians 5:17). The flesh desires what is contrary to the Holy Spirit, and the flesh often wins this internal tug-of-war. Peter warns that Satan lies in wait like a fierce lion seeking to devour us (1 Peter 5:8). Yet we walk as though we weren't in danger, often putting ourselves in positions of peril where we're vulnerable to attack. How do we successfully wage war against our spiritual enemies?

James 4:7-10 prescribes winning tactics for the fight. As in all spiritual things, the power is God's rather than ours, but our role isn't passive.

First, we must submit to God. This is not a periodic act, but a constant posture. The Greek verb in 4:7 translated as "submit" means "to line up under." It was often used in classical Greek with respect to military order; soldiers were to line up under superior officers. In the New Testament, the term refers almost universally to being under the authority of Jesus Christ. The world, the flesh, and the devil do not value submission. The world applauds independent people who wear no one's yoke. The flesh chafes at submission to anything outside itself. Satan tempts us all as he tempted Christ, with self-indulgence and personal power (Matthew 4:1-11). But God calls us to submission.

When we submit to God, we're under his tender care and protection. As soon as we walk outside of that submission, we're in danger of succumbing to our adversaries. The first step in spiritual warfare is not aggressively moving toward the enemy, but meekly yielding to the one who fights for us (Exodus 14:14).

How do we submit? We seek God through his word. I cannot emphasize enough the need for every Christian to spend significant time in God's word—in the Bible itself, rather than just books about it. There's no substitute for studying, memorizing, and meditating on God's direct communication to his people. When we know the Bible, we can pattern our lives after God's word rather than in ways that come more naturally to us.

We also submit through prayer, in hearing godly teaching, and in Christian fellowship. We submit by confessing our sin and repenting from it. We submit by sacrificing our personal ambitions, our time, and our treasure in service to God. We submit by loving and serving others rather than ourselves, laying down our lives for our brothers and sisters (1 John 3:16). If this sounds less like fighting than surrendering, it is. The first step in spiritual warfare is to surrender to the good King we serve. The winning battle begins on our knees.

In his classic work *Sit, Walk, Stand*, Watchman Nee noted that our spiritual formation must begin from a position of sitting in the heavenly places with Christ.[49] Only when we sit can we effectively walk with him and stand firm in our struggle against the devil. James's prescription for successful spiritual warfare also begins from that position. We must first submit, acknowledging our utter dependence on a good and all-powerful God before stepping toward the fight.

Once we're in a posture of submission to God, we can resist. We resist the lies of Satan with the truths of God. There are two primary names used in the New Testament for our chief adversary. The Greek word translated in James 4:7 as "devil" is *diabolos*, which means accuser, whereas the word translated as "Satan" means adversary. In Genesis, Job, Zechariah, Revelation, and many other places in Scripture, we see the *diabolos* in his role as accuser, acting like a cosmic prosecutor before the judgment seat of God. In the devil's first appearance in Scripture, he accuses God of withholding a good gift. Eve believed the accusation and took hold of the one thing prohibited to her, seeking to be her own god rather than remain submitted to the true God. And so paradise was lost.

Many of us struggle against internal, accusing, and self-condemning voices. We can mistake these accusations for righteous conviction, but the Holy Spirit's conviction is precise, founded on Scripture, and useful in prompting repentance. The accusations of the devil are general, producing only a sense of condemnation, worthlessness, and hopelessness. Sometimes he accuses with respect to old sins long ago forgiven, questioning God's complete forgiveness. Condemnation has the ironic result of producing more sin, because we hear the accusing voice and we conclude, "That's who I am; it's what I do." The accusations are based on just enough truth to stick and encumber our walk.

The prophet Zechariah experienced the following vision concerning a trial before the one righteous Judge:

> Then he showed me Joshua the high priest standing before the angel of the Lord, and Satan standing at his right hand to accuse him. The Lord said to Satan, "The Lord rebuke you, Satan! Indeed, the Lord who has chosen Jerusalem rebuke you! Is this not a brand plucked from the fire?" Now Joshua was clothed with filthy garments and standing before the angel. He spoke and said to those who were standing before him, saying, "Remove the filthy garments from him." Again he said to him, "See, I have taken your iniquity away from you and will clothe you with festal robes." Then I said, "Let them put a clean turban on his head." So they put a clean turban on his head and clothed him with garments, while the angel of the Lord was standing by. (Zechariah 3:1-5)

The devil can only accuse and destroy. Our Father in heaven redeems and creates. When we submit to God, he protects us from accusation because we've taken on Christ's righteousness as our own. We put on his festal robes, and these, rather than our filthy garments, are what God sees. God judges us based on the righteousness he has joyfully bestowed on us in Christ. The enemy would have us labor under crippling, generalized guilt that produces no good fruit. God calls us to freedom in Christ, embracing a good gift freely given. Resist the devil with the truth that God has imputed Christ's righteousness to you, and the devil and his accusations will flee.

When we're submitted to God and in the midst of the resistance against the adversary, we're to draw near to God and he'll draw near to us. God is sometimes quiet, but he's never far and never absent. God's character is revealed in ancient words spoken by a prophet of God: "The Lord is with you when you are with him. And if you seek him, he will let you find him" (2 Chronicles 15:2).

How do we draw near to God? As with any other relationship, we spend intentional, undistracted time with him. In challenging seasons of life where I've particularly needed to draw near to God, I increase my time in the Bible and in prayer. I sometimes fast, and I limit my exposure to media and listen only to music that exalts God. I surround myself with people who'll speak truth to me. I attend midweek worship services more frequently. To some, this will smack of legalism, but these are practical steps we can take to draw near to God. If we grow distant in a relationship with another person, we cannot correct that distance with mere sentiment and good intention. We succeed only when we devote more time and attention to the relationship, being amply free to both speak and to listen. So it is with God. As Christ himself promised, "Seek and you will find" (Matthew 7:7). Though it's good to draw near to God in seasons of distress, it's far better to experience that closeness as part of our daily discipline.

In the fight against our enemies, we must be pure. James calls sinners to cleanse their hands and the double-minded to purify their hearts. He's calling out both observable sin and our invisible, sinful thoughts. We cannot expect to wage war successfully against the enemies of God if we're holding on to sin. Are you stealing? Steal no more and return what you've taken. Are you adulterous? Confess and repent. Are you prideful? Serve people who have no capacity to return anything to you, so you can grow in humility. Are you greedy? Give your money away.

We cannot simultaneously protect cherished sins and guard our hearts. If we continue in sin without repentance, the battle is lost. As western Christians, many of us have lost the urgency of living a godly life, but this is not the Christianity of the Bible. Persons who persist in unrepentant sin show that they're not Christians at all, and are in danger of hell (Hebrews 10:26; 2 Peter 2:20; Romans 11:20-22; Matthew 7:21-23; John 15:6; 1 John 3:6-10; 1 Corinthians 9:26–10:12; Galatians 5:19-24).

Of course, none of us is without sin. In his mercy, God doesn't generally reveal all our sin to us at once. As we mature, he exposes new layers of sin for which we need to repent. He often begins by convicting us with respect to the open, obvious, and destructive sins of the flesh, and then moves to dealing with the more subtle attitudes of the heart. Even when we've matured, we can lapse into old notorious sins if we're not vigilant. We cannot expect to prevail in our fight against the adversary if we're clinging to sin.

Righteousness has gone out of vogue, even within the church. This is tragic, and it has served to diminish the church's influence on this earth. We tolerate sin in ourselves and laugh at it in others. With regard to certain sins—like greed and sexual impurity—we often enshrine sin and call it good! James calls us to a very different attitude. With regard to our sin, we're to be miserable and mourn and weep. Yes, God forgives us, but sin still has consequences. Sin still wounds. Sin still creates distance in our relationship with God. Sin still grieves our heavenly Father. Sin still impairs our witness. The wages of sin is still death—death of joy, death of peace, death of intimacy (Romans 6:23). Paul warns that we're all servants; the question is, Which master will we serve? It will be either sin or godly righteousness (Romans 6:16).

In 2 Corinthians, Paul refers to an earlier letter he'd sent to the Corinthian church in which he'd challenged them with regard to their sin. This earlier letter had caused the church much sorrow, and Paul didn't regret it. His letter had its intended result, but Paul clarifies that he doesn't take delight in sorrow alone, but in the repentance that such sorrow produces. "I now rejoice, not that you were made sorrowful, but that you were made sorrowful to the point of repentance.... For the sorrow that is according to the will of God produces a repentance without regret" (2 Corinthians 7:9-10).

James's last instruction in this section is that we humble ourselves, allowing God to lift us up. To humble ourselves is to make ourselves low, to recognize that we're creatures in the presence of our sovereign Creator. Such a posture is anathema in a world whose highest values are self-adulation and self-fulfillment. The kingdom of God operates under a very different value system.

God repeats this theme throughout Scripture. Jesus says that whoever humbles himself as a child will be greatest in the kingdom of heaven (Matthew 18:4). He says also that everyone who exalts himself will be humbled, and whoever humbles himself will be exalted (Luke 14:11). Peter instructs us to humble ourselves under the mighty hand of God, who will then lift us up (1 Peter 5:6). We must say, as John the Baptist said in regard to Jesus, "He must increase, but I must decrease" (John 3:30). The glory that flows from such humility is true and eternal, as opposed to the baseless, ephemeral glories offered by this world.

Discussions of spiritual warfare can be self-glorifying, creating the impression that God provides a source of power for his children to wield in service of their own goals and purposes. Such a fight is lost before it begins because its very aim is contrary to God's intentions. We live and we fight in service to a good king, and his ambition is that we be conformed to the image of Jesus Christ. Submit to the king in humility, resist his enemy, repent of your sin—and he will lift you up. The reward is intimacy with Christ and the unparalleled joy of eternal fellowship with our good king.

Discussion Questions

1. Have you ever experienced spiritual warfare? If so, when? If not, do you believe spiritual warfare exists?
2. With respect to spiritual warfare, we looked in this chapter at tactics of submission, purity, and humility. Do you think these are effective tactics? Which of these do you find most challenging to utilize?
3. In the realm of spiritual warfare, what does victory look like?

22

DO NOT JUDGE

Do not speak against one another, brethren.
He who speaks against a brother or judges his brother,
speaks against the law and judges the law;
but if you judge the law, you are not a doer
of the law but a judge of it.
There is only one Lawgiver and Judge,
the One who is able to save and to destroy;
but who are you who judge your neighbor?

JAMES 4:11-12

One of Jesus's most famous teachings is "Do not judge so that you will not be judged" (Matthew 7:1). In fact, this statement seems to represent the sum total of many people's knowledge of Christ's teaching. It may be the most quoted passage in Scripture—and the most misapplied.

James 4:11-12 echoes Christ's command that we shouldn't judge. Some people think this means they can do whatever they want, and no one should criticize their behavior. But those people don't really believe that nothing can be labeled bad or good. Just watch how those same people react when someone steals their stuff, keys their car, or criticizes them. If "Do not judge" means that we can't call anything bad or good, then we can't even criticize someone for judging.

So what do Jesus and James mean when they say, "Do not judge"?

James is writing to Christians, so he's identifying a problem within the church. These Christians were speaking ill of one another and judging one another. We don't know exactly what prompted this behavior, but something was happening in the church to elicit judgment. Some believers were adhering to a standard that others were not, and the resulting whispers of condemnation were tearing down the church's unity. Sadly, this situation isn't difficult for us to imagine because it's not far from our experience. There's nothing new under the sun.

Our interpretation of this teaching of James, and of Christ's teaching from Matthew 7, often depends on where we fall along the spectrum between legalism and licentiousness. You might say, "Well, I don't want to be either of those things, because neither one sounds very good!" You're right.

Allow me to use this spectrum to tell a story. It's a story I'd rather not tell, but as Paul says in 2 Corinthians, "I will delight in my weaknesses for Christ's sake, for when I am weak, then I am strong" (2 Corinthians 12:10).

I attended a Christian college. Though not nearly as strict as some Christian colleges, it had more rules governing moral behavior than you'd find at a secular university. For example, drinking alcohol on campus or having a girl in your dorm room outside of visiting hours were punishable offenses.

There were very few people in our school who didn't profess Christianity. Broadly speaking, there were three groups of people within this Christian community: the legalists, the licentious, and what I call the lovely. After a few minutes of observation, a visitor to our dining hall could draw neat geographic lines between the first two groups because they never sat at the same tables. The legalists were called the God squad. The God squad eagerly attended mandatory chapels and convocations while the licentious persistently lobbied the administration to get rid of the requirement. The God squad studiously adhered to the rules while the licentious found creative ways in which to violate them. The God squad prided itself on purity while the licentious prided themselves on authenticity.

Predictably, those two groups didn't like each other. It could be ugly. They often spoke ill of each other, sometimes bitterly. The God squad condemned the unrighteous behavior of the licentious, while the licentious condemned the hypocrisy of Christians who professed to be saved by grace but who lived and spoke as though moral uprightness was all that mattered. Members of the God squad would hear that a member of the licentious group had been disciplined for some infraction and receive it with thinly disguised glee.

Then there was the third set of people, those I call the lovely. This was the smallest group. They lived righteously and didn't wink at sin, but they loved people from the licentious group. They were more difficult to identify in the dining hall because they often moved between groups. Both factions sought these people for their wisdom and because they were safe and gentle. The lovely derived their sense of security and identity from Christ's accomplished work and not from their own moral performance. The lovely were indeed righteous because they eagerly longed to please the God they loved.

You might be wondering which group I was in. This is where my story becomes painful to tell. For my first three years, I was firmly in the God squad camp—morally upright and critical of those who were not. I remember with sadness my smug sense of moral superiority and the intense desire I had for control. I feared the licentiousness of other people, especially those who claimed to be Christians. I liked rules and I liked people who adhered to them, because that made my world more predictable and controllable.

In my senior year, I transitioned—not to the lovely, and not exactly to the licentious. Instead I became that most noxious of things, a hypocrite. I became the sort of person for whom Christ reserved his harshest criticism. I sat at the God squad table, but secretly behaved like the licentious. I engaged in the same behavior I condemned in others. I was the opposite of lovely.

As I left the cloistered environment of a Christian college and went to a large secular university for law school, I was less judgmental of other people's moral infractions, but more fully engaged in my own fleshly pursuits. What might surprise you is that I never wavered in my belief in God. I didn't reject him, and in fact pursued him. I attended the same church I attend today. I found myself looking back over the fence at the person I was before—a legalist—and I loathed that. I didn't want to return to it. But at the time I failed to recognize the possibility of a third way, the lovely way.

"How could this happen?" you probably ask. How could I move so far from one end of the spectrum to the other?

Actually, the journey from legalism to licentiousness isn't far at all. In the political context, parties moving further to the left or to the right don't move along a plane but along the diameter of a circle. As they go far enough, they meet and look the same—resulting in authoritarian dictatorships. Similarly, legalism and licentiousness are far more similar than they initially appear. They both derive their identity in the flesh. The legalist says, "Do not handle, do not taste, do not touch" (Colossians 2:21). Paul says that this way of thinking is false wisdom and false humility, and it's destined to perish; it's a denial of our participation in Christ's death (Colossians 2:16-23). The licentious person says, "I'll sin more, so that grace will abound" (Romans 6:1). Paul says that such people are enslaved to sin, and he asks, "What benefit were you then deriving from the things of which you are now ashamed?" (Romans 6:21). Neither sort of person is living as God intends for them to live, and each kind looks at the other and judges.

Sin has natural consequences, and I suffered mine. I won't bore you with all my stories, but one is both amusing and sad. In law school, I took a course in law and religion, focusing on the evolution of U.S. constitutional law governing church-state relations. It was a fascinating class that I took in the spring semester of my final year. I loved that class, but on a dare from a classmate, I brought beer to class one day and drank it just to see what the professor might do. My friend was supposed to join me, but he demurred, so I was the lone drinker that day.

Most law school courses are based 100 percent on the final exam, which is one of the reasons law school can be so stressful; one bad test day can derail an entire semester of effort. But this class was different, and a significant part of our grade depended on class participation, which was at the professor's discretion. I was a star student, eagerly reading and contributing to conversations in class. I was easily the most engaged student in a class where many others didn't even bother to show up. But I disrespected the professor that day, and in the end he gave me a C for the course.

As I approached graduation, I was negotiating with a firm about a job, and their offer was conditioned on my graduating "with distinction," which required a certain GPA. I missed that GPA by a tenth of a point, and I graduated right into unemployment.

Prompted in part by my job search frustrations, my sin accelerated. After a few months, I crashed. I was saddled with tremendous law school debt, I had no income to speak of, I was lonely, and my parents were on the mission field with little spare cash for their now twenty-four-year-old son. More significant, however, is that by God's grace I'd come into a crushing awareness of the depths of my sin. I was grieved and repentant. It was a painful season. Yet to the extent I'm at all lovely today, that period of suffering was a critical season for my growth. In that moment of pain, I started to piece together who I really was in Christ.

Why do I tell this story? Because I want you to know I've spent time on both sides of the legalist-licentious divide, and neither side is where I want to be.

"Do not slander one another." The prohibition is clear, and yet we do it. We gossip, we condemn, and we murder with our speech. This isn't reserved for the legalists. Some of the most self-righteous people I've encountered are those who tend to be licentious, and who seem to think that spiritual authenticity is measured by the audacity of sin. They look with open contempt on those who are pure in their conduct.

James tells us that anyone who speaks against his brother or judges him, speaks against the law and judges it. The wording is confusing, in part because we don't know exactly what "law" James is referring to. The Greek word's meaning is broad enough to refer to different kinds of statutes or commands or principles. One possibility is that James is referencing the Mosaic law, which provides that we shouldn't hate or slander our brother (Leviticus 19:15-18). Or he may be referencing Christ's command recorded in Matthew, where Jesus tells us not to judge. (James wouldn't have had Matthew's Gospel, but he would have known Jesus's teaching on the topic.)

We can also look to how James uses the word "law" elsewhere in this letter, such as where he references the "law of liberty" in 1:25 and 2:12. This law of liberty is the law of the gospel; it's the fact of Christ's sacrifice on the cross redeeming us from the curse of the law. We're saved not by our works, but by the grace provided through Christ's atoning work. When we condemn others based on their behavior rather than through the prism of the cross, we're judging that law. James also speaks of the "royal law" in 2:8, where he tells us to love our neighbors as ourselves, which is inconsistent with judging and slandering our neighbor.

All these definitions of law point to one truth—when we speak ill of our brother and judge him for breaking the law, we're in the process of breaking the law ourselves. In the instant we slander, we also become hypocrites, because we're breaking the very law we're claiming to uphold.

I identify three commands that are stated or implied in James 4:11-12:

(1) *Stop speaking ill of one another.* You and your brothers and sisters in Christ have equal standing before the Lord. In slandering one another, you're tearing down the church and breaking the unity God longs for us to have with one another (John 17). The world can know we're followers of Christ by our love for one another, and speaking poorly of one another is not loving.

(2) *Stop making up new laws.* James says there's only one Lawgiver, and yet we make up our own laws because we like the sense of control that laws bring. I'm not talking about the civil laws necessary for the governance of a country or a community, but about religious rules—the extrabiblical standards we create so we can measure who's in and who's out of God's kingdom.

Each generation has its own set of such rules. In Paul's day, it was eating meat sacrificed to idols. That rule isn't in the front of our minds today, but we have plenty other rules of our own. New rules are the stock in trade of the legalist and the hypocrite. In Jesus's polemic against the Pharisees, he says these religious teachers "tie up heavy loads and lay them on men's shoulders, but they themselves are unwilling to move them with so much as a finger" (Matthew 23:4).

There is one Lawgiver. We must avoid creating any spiritual standards that aren't clearly expressed in Scripture where the one Lawgiver has already issued the entirety of his commands.

(3) *Stop judging.* It isn't judging for us to say that lying or stealing is wrong, because the one Lawgiver has already declared those things wrong. The same goes for anything else God has identified as sin. But it is judging for me to create new standards of conduct so I can judge those who fall short. It's also judging to say, "He's not a good Christian because he….." Or, "I don't think he's a Christian at all, because I saw him do….." Moral performance isn't what makes us Christians; Jesus makes us Christians, and only Jesus gets to judge who's in and who's out of his kingdom.

There is one Lawgiver and one Judge. When we set ourselves up as lawgiver or judge, we thus encroach on the exclusive domain of God, and are guilty of a clear sin.

The world is not short of slander, self-righteousness, or judgment. It's woefully short of loveliness. We'll find it impossible to be lovely in this world unless we derive our spiritual security and sense of identity from the accomplished work of Christ rather than from our own performance. When we rest in Christ's accomplished work, as we're called to do, loveliness springs from us because Christ is in us. The flesh has been crucified and it's no longer we who live, but Christ living in us (Galatians 2:20). When we no longer derive our identity from fleshly accomplishment, we're free to love because we're no longer judging and no longer comparing. This is an area in which virtually all of us have room to repent. I encourage you to join me in asking God to reveal to you where you're falling short in this, and seek his great grace in moving you toward loveliness.

Discussion Questions

1. We can probably all recall people who've influenced our walk with Christ who fit into each of the three categories—legalist, licentious, and lovely. Try to recall someone who fits in the lovely group. Why do you see that person as such?

2. How are the legalists and licentious actually similar?

3. Consider the parable of the prodigal son (Luke 15:11-32). Are all three groups—legalist, licentious, and lovely— represented in that story? How so? What would it take for each of the brothers to become "lovely"?

4. After reading this chapter, how does James 4:11-12 challenge you regarding the condition of your own heart?

23

AN OPEN HAND
OR A CLOSED FIST?

Come now, you who say, "Today or tomorrow we will go to
such and such a city, and spend a year there and engage in
business and make a profit." Yet you do not know what your life
will be like tomorrow. You are just a vapor that appears for a little
while and then vanishes away. Instead, you ought to say,
"If the Lord wills, we will live and also do this or that."
But as it is, you boast in your arrogance; all such boasting is evil.
Therefore, to one who knows the right thing to do
and does not do it, to him it is sin.

JAMES 4:13-17

Almost every day at work, I receive Microsoft Outlook meeting invitations from someone proposing a time and place for a meeting. I have the option to "Accept" or "Decline." As someone who grew up knowing James 4:13-17, I've wished there were also this option: "If the Lord wills it." Some small part of me feels presumptuous in clicking "Accept."

But there's more to this passage than simply saying the words "If the Lord wills" when we're announcing our plans. James isn't calling us to window-dress an arrogant heart with hollow words. The essence of James's teaching is that Christians must embrace the supremacy and sovereignty of God in their lives.

As we've seen, James had profound concerns about his readers' relationship with money. In chapter 1, he says that the poor man will be exalted while the rich man fades away. He devoted the first part of chapter 2 to the sin of partiality, criticizing the church for treating rich people better than poor people. In chapter 4, he identifies the desire for material pleasures as the source of quarrels and conflicts among people in the church. Later, in chapter 5, he'll tell the rich people of this world to weep and mourn, because their very riches will serve as a witness against them. For James's readers, the relentless pursuit of money—and the place held by money in their hearts—was damaging the community of the church, distracting people from the pursuit of true wisdom, and making them ineffective in serving God.

James 4:13-17 also relates to money. People in the church were arrogantly announcing their plans to engage in business and make a profit. Taking this in light of what James says throughout the letter, we see that money was more than a mere distraction to these Christians. It was, in fact, an idol.

The brash, confident individualist is highly esteemed in America. The risk-taker, the innovator, and the money-maker are icons of our culture. Business is something we think we do really well. We also place a high value on self-confidence, personified in the assertive, tough-talking self-made man. We lionize the person who can take the bull by the horns, wrestle it to the ground, put his brand on it, and say, "Look what I did!" Seeing the self-made man who seems to carry no one's yoke, a lot of us think, "I wish I could be more like that." But James suggests that God has a different view of this guy. Rather than call him "confident,"

James might use the word "arrogant." Rather than admiring his boasting, James might call it evil.

It's not evil to take risks, to innovate, or to exercise competence in the world of commerce. But it's arrogant to boast of control we don't really possess. And it's evil to elevate our own ambitions above the plans God has for us.

The character James describes here is familiar to us, possibly because we see him in the mirror. We boldly announce where we're going, what we're going to do, and the money we're going to make. We might give lip service to honoring God in what we do, but our plans are our own, like the money we expect to make from them. As common as this is, it isn't good. There are certain sins we see in our culture that horrify us. Other sins are so culturally ingrained that we don't even recognize them as sin. But Scripture, not our culture, defines the appropriate attitude toward our plans and our money. According to the Bible, the right thing to do with respect to both plans and money is to hold them with an open hand, acknowledging that God can fill or empty that hand as he wills.

In Luke, Jesus used a parable to teach a similar lesson to the one James presents in this passage.

Then he said to them, "Beware, and be on your guard against every form of greed; for not even when one has an abundance does his life consist of his possessions." And he told them a parable, saying, "The land of a rich man was very productive. And he began reasoning to himself, saying, 'What shall I do, since I have no place to store my crops?' Then he said, 'This is what I will do: I will tear down my barns and build larger ones, and there I will store all my grain and my goods. And I will say to my soul, Soul, you have many goods laid up for many years to come; take your ease, eat, drink and be merry.' But God said to him, 'You fool! This very night your soul is required of you; and now who will own what you have prepared?'" (Luke 12:18-20)

The man in Jesus's parable was prospering. Today, we'd probably look at him and say, "Wow! That guy is really blessed." His chief anxiety was having enough space to put all his stuff. I've seen similar anxiety in my law practice when a client comes into a lot of money after a deal closes, and he has to figure out where he's going to put all his newfound cash. You might be surprised at how anxiety-producing it is to come into significant wealth. The man in Jesus's parable had no idea that his very life was about to be extinguished. What use would barns full of grain be to a dead man who left it all behind?

The Bible's teaching on money doesn't mean we shouldn't plan, save, or be wise with our finances. But to a far greater degree than we appreciate, the Bible teaches that money has great potential to corrupt our hearts. Most of us are guilty of looking to money rather than to God to provide for our needs. The level of passion, vigor, and trust we evidence toward money should be reserved for God alone. Most of us hold our money with a closed fist, not an open hand.

Holding tightly to our money and our plans is sowing to the flesh, which produces idolatry, enmity, strife, dissension, factions, and envy. Our love for money—the very thing we're counting on to bring us joy—is the thing keeping us from it. But sowing to the Spirit means acknowledging that every tomorrow is a gift of God, and that every dollar put in our hands is God's, both to give and to take. This produces love, joy, peace, patience, kindness, goodness, faithfulness, gentleness, and self-control.

So what, you might ask, should that rich man actually have done with his crops? He probably should have given away the excess. His existing barns were likely sufficient to store reasonable reserves for the year to come, and he could have trusted God to provide the next harvest. The rich man's greatest sin, however, was not in building bigger barns, but in letting his life consist of his possessions. Possessions were his passion, his god, and the thing in which he placed his trust. Note his words: "Soul, you have many goods laid up for many years to come; take your ease, eat, drink, and be merry." He was looking to material possessions for spiritual sustenance. Acquisition was his life orientation.

The rich man was holding onto his life with a closed fist. Christ calls us to the opposite—the openhanded approach:

If anyone wishes to come after Me, he must deny himself, and take up his cross and follow Me. For whoever wishes to save his life will lose it; but whoever loses his life for My sake will find it. For what will it profit a man if he gains the whole world and forfeits his soul? Or what will a man give in exchange for his soul? For the Son of Man is going to come in the glory of his Father with his angels, and will the repay every man according to his deeds. (Matthew 16:24-27)

The apostle Paul exemplifies the openhanded approach to life:

Now I rejoice in my sufferings for your sake, and in my flesh I do my share on behalf of his body, which is the church, in filling up what is lacking in Christ's afflictions. (Colossians 1:24)

Can we, like Paul, rejoice when our plans are thwarted by suffering? Paul was able to rejoice because he acknowledged God's supreme role in his life. His driving passion was to proclaim Christ in service to Christ's body, which is the church. Do we share Paul's passion? Or does the desire to serve ourselves consume us? A life lived in service to self will bring despair rather than fulfillment.

Think of the most powerful Christian biographies you've read. How many of those stories of significant lives involved the uninterrupted completion of well-laid plans? Probably none. How many stories involved unwelcome life events that no one would ever choose? Almost all of them.

We learn the openhanded approach to life through suffering. Without it, we easily conclude that the best things in life are the fleeting things of this earth. Only in the cauldron of suffering do we recognize that there must be something higher, better, and more enduring than the hollow promises of financial security.

The application of this passage involves far more than simply uttering the words, "If God wills." James calls us to genuinely submit our plans to God. This requires the subordination of our goals to God's intentions for us. It includes more than praying about our plans; it also involves not despairing when those plans are involuntarily changed. The openhanded approach to life requires faith, because we have to trust the one who puts in and takes out of our open hand. We don't know whether we have a tomorrow on this earth, but if we have one, let's go forward with an openness to God's plans rather than the close-fisted approach of demanding what we think is ours. We might be surprised to experience the joy that flows from dependence on God.

Everything we are and everything we have is God's, including our money and our tomorrows. This is cause not for despair, but for rejoicing, because we serve a good Father who has gladly chosen to give us an eternal kingdom where moth and rust don't destroy, and where thieves never break in and steal. If you're suffering today because of unrealized ambitions or frustrated plans, I encourage you to rejoice in your suffering, as Paul rejoiced in his. Because tribulation brings about perseverance, and perseverance builds proven character, and proven character brings hope—hope which does not disappoint.

Discussion Questions

1. What part of this chapter was most thought-provoking for you, or personally challenging. Why?
2. In this chapter we observed that holding tightly onto our money and our plans is "sowing to the flesh," which produces idolatry, enmity, strife, dissension, factions, and envy. How can you honestly evaluate or determine whether this describes you?
3. Reread James 4:16-17. God obviously takes our arrogant boasting seriously. Why do you think he does—and why do you think we so often don't?

24

RICHES

Come now, you rich, weep and howl for your miseries
which are coming upon you. Your riches have rotted and
your garments have become moth-eaten. Your gold and
your silver have rusted; and their rust will be a witness
against you and will consume your flesh like fire. It is in
the last days that you have stored up your treasure!
Behold, the pay of the laborers who mowed your fields,
and which has been withheld by you, cries out against you;
and the outcry of those who did the harvesting has reached
the ears of the Lord of Sabaoth. You have lived luxuriously
on the earth and led a life of wanton pleasure; you have
fattened your hearts in a day of slaughter. You have condemned
and put to death the righteous man; he does not resist you.

JAMES 5:1-6

We're resourceful apologists when it comes to the Bible's teaching on the dangers of wealth. When we encounter a passage like James 5:1-6, we reflexively explain why it doesn't apply to us. We assume such passages must refer to someone richer or meaner than we are. But that approach to Scripture has contributed to endemic idolatry. We give lip service to a sovereign God who provides all our needs according to his riches in glory, while we live as though money is our sustenance and hope. If a god is defined as the object of our primary hope, and for which we make our greatest sacrifices—then money is indeed the prevailing American god.

Apologists for wealth argue that the Bible doesn't condemn money. They describe the virtue of Lydia, the seller of purple described in Acts 16 who was a wealthy church member. They point out that in 1 Timothy, Paul refers to *love* of money—not money itself—as the root of evil. They emphasize the Bible's wisdom literature that speaks about working hard to earn money, and about the value of saving and financial discipline. They'll point out that James 5:1-6 refers to people withholding wages and putting righteous people to death—which can't mean us!

When we're confronted with a challenging passage of Scripture, we often jump to what it *doesn't* mean before, with reflection, we discover what it clearly *does* mean. So before we dismiss the applicability of this passage in James to our own lives, let's allow his words to sink in, and evaluate both our conduct and the state of our heart with regard to money. If we don't see ourselves in this passage, it's quite possible we're just using a bad mirror.

James felt no compulsion to cushion the blow of his harsh words. Like a parent raising his voice to a child on the precipice of danger, James sounds an alarm to change his readers' hearts. James knew that the love of money was corrupting his audience and destroying their witness and community. If his words make you uncomfortable, they're having their intended effect.

James stands conventional wisdom on its head. Conventional wisdom dictates that we welcome wealth as a blessing, while James says that the rich should weep and howl at the miseries coming upon them. Conventional wisdom suggests that wealth provides security, while James says that wealth decays. Conventional wisdom argues that wealth is evidence of merit, while James says that wealth testifies against the wealthy. Conventional wisdom sees luxury as a worthy goal, while James says that living a life of indulgence leads to death and judgment. Do we believe the Bible's teaching on the topic of money? Are we as believers any less addicted to the pursuit of wealth and leisure than people who aren't Christians? Are our dreams and ambitions any less tied to wealth than those of the rest of the world?

James isn't alone in his warnings about wealth. Consider these teachings from Jesus and Paul:

Do not store up for yourselves treasures on earth, where moth and rust destroy, and where thieves break in and steal. But store up for yourselves treasures in heaven, where neither moth nor rust destroys, and where thieves do not break in or steal; for where your treasure is, there your heart will be also. (Matthew 6:19-21)

But woe to you who are rich, for you have already received your comfort. (Luke 6:24)

Those who want to get rich fall into temptation and a snare and many foolish and harmful desires which plunge men into ruin and destruction. For the love of money is a root of all sorts of evil, and some by longing for it have wandered away from the faith and pierced themselves with many griefs. (1 Timothy 6:9-10)

Instruct those who are rich in this present world not to be conceited or to fix their hope on the uncertainty of riches, but on God, who richly supplies us with all things to enjoy. Instruct them to do good, to be rich in good works, to be generous and ready to share, storing up for themselves the treasure of a good foundation for the future, so that they may take hold of that which is life indeed. (1 Timothy 6:17-19)

Spiritual charlatans enrich themselves by selling the lie that our wealth is God's chief desire for his children, and that such wealth is evidence of God's favor. These teachers are popular because they appeal to our flesh, but their teachings contradict God's word. The Bible consistently warns the rich and condemns a lifestyle oriented toward luxury.

Wealth is dangerous. It's dangerous whether we have it or merely desire it. It never delivers what it promises, and it easily displaces God's rightful place as our single hope and source of provision.

The passages above teach us that love of wealth:

> displaces future, eternal comforts;
> plunges men into ruin and destruction;
> causes people to wander from the faith;
> pierces us with many griefs; and
> is of no eternal value.

Do we actually believe all this? Or do we continue to slavishly pursue wealth as if it were worthy of our trust? This is at the core of James's letter. He's asking us what we really believe, and challenging us to evidence genuine belief with a changed life.

James describes the types of conduct that grow from love of wealth. Recipients of his letter were withholding wages from workers. They had also caused righteous men to be put to death. We don't know more detail, and commentaries disagree as to whether James is referencing specific events. But these are natural consequences of addiction to wealth. Wealth brings power and influence. When that wealth and power are challenged, the wealth-infatuated heart flames with fear of loss and unrighteous indignation. In reaction to threats against their wealth, the wealthy often respond with oppression and violence.

Before we exclude ourselves from this description, we should ask ourselves questions like these: Do I leverage my financial position to gain advantage over those who have less? Do I pay my employees a fair wage? Are my views on public policy derived purely from their effect on my wallet? Do I view the poor with compassion or contempt? Would I rather sue a Christian brother in court than suffer financial loss? Is my personal wealth a higher priority than helping those in need?

The chief sin pertaining to wealth is that we trust in it rather than in God. Having wealth allows us to mimic faith without actually having to trust in God at all. Having wealth allows us to live a life in which genuine belief is unnecessary because we've hedged all our bets.

God is to be our first love. To seek another source for our comfort and sustenance is adultery. As in human relationships, our relationship with God will be weak and distant if we're unfaithful to him. God's tenderness underlies his commands about wealth; God cares very much for the condition of our hearts. He knows fully what we find hard to believe: that love of wealth creates tremendous grief and deprives us of perfect peace. God desires higher things for us.

I see myself in this passage. I want to live the very life James condemns, a life of ease and visible resources. I would rather depend on a robust bank account balance than on a God who's invisible. I want the both/and of a fat wallet and godly character.

My desire for earthly comfort often causes my heart to drift; it displaces my first love, which brings on anxiety. I know my seasons of greatest dependence have also been my times of greatest intimacy with Christ, but I'm more angry than grateful when I anticipate lack. I justify myself, noting how others are far wealthier and less generous than I am, and this justification short-circuits my repentance. But I'm growing in this, and I repent again today. Tomorrow, perhaps, I'll have to repent again.

The world's system puts us on a treadmill. We're constantly running to accumulate more, yet failing to get anywhere we really want to go. Peace eludes us. The beautiful irony is that when we get off that treadmill and instead rest in the presence of our good Father, we receive an enduring peace. Paul described such a rightly oriented life as "that which is life indeed." As always, God's perfect gifts far exceed the false promises of this earth.

Discussion Questions

1. Who do you think James is addressing in 5:1-6?
2. If asked whether they trust more in money or in God, most Christians know the "right" answer. But if someone were to closely observe your life, what would your choices and emotions reveal as the true object of your trust?
3. What practical, tangible steps can Christians take to cultivate trust in God rather than in wealth?

25

BE PATIENT

Therefore be patient, brethren, until the coming of the Lord.
The farmer waits for the precious produce of the soil,
being patient about it, until it gets the early and late rains.
You too be patient; strengthen your hearts, for the coming of the
Lord is near. Do not complain, brethren, against one another,
so that you yourselves may not be judged;
behold, the Judge is standing right at the door.

JAMES 5:7-9

The spirit of this age prompts me to fret. Our culture is becoming increasingly polarized, and people of differing opinions seem incapable of reasonable debate in good faith. For all the popular talk of love, tolerance, and inclusion, we seem to be getting angrier and increasingly unable to deal with each other with civility.

What's particularly distressing is that Christians seem to be in the crosshairs of the people with the megaphones. Despite the fact that Christian faith introduced the world to the radical ideas of human dignity and equality across racial and economic differences, the world unfairly derides Christianity as bigoted. The profound dysfunction of the world cries out for spiritual solutions, yet the world increasingly rejects God. We seem to be living out the apostle Paul's prophetic words in Romans:

> Furthermore, just as they did not think it worthwhile to retain the knowledge of God, so God gave them over to a depraved mind, so that they do what ought not to be done. They have become filled with every kind of wickedness, evil, greed and depravity. They are full of envy, murder, strife, deceit and malice. They are gossips, slanderers, God-haters, insolent, arrogant and boastful; they invent ways of doing evil; they disobey their parents; they have no understanding, no fidelity, no love, no mercy. Although they know God's righteous decree that those who do such things deserve death, they not only continue to do these very things but also approve of those who practice them. (Romans 1:28-32)

It's hard to see a way back for this world, and sometimes the future can look frightening. How are Christians supposed to speak, react, and order their lives in this hostile world? Can we navigate this new age without compromising the purity of our faith?

James was writing to people undergoing a far more unsettling season than we face now. He was writing to the "the twelve tribes who are dispersed abroad." These were Jews who'd previously lived in Jerusalem, but were driven out of their homes and dispersed around the Mediterranean because of their profession of Christ. Christians were pariahs in their Jerusalem homeland and objects of suspicion in the balance of the Roman Empire. Some of them had managed to flee Jerusalem with their wealth intact, but the day would soon come when Christians throughout the Roman Empire would be intensely persecuted for refusing to acknowledge Caesar as God. The Christians to whom James was writing would be increasingly hated because they loved Jesus.

In the midst of this trying time, James didn't counsel a coup, a lobbying effort, or organized military resistance. In fact, he devoted significant ink to criticizing his audience for relying on earthly forms of power, most particularly wealth. Instead, James counseled patience, and warned his readers not to turn against one another in the midst of the persecution.

James 5:7 begins with "Therefore," which directs us to look at the preceding passage for help in interpreting this one. What came immediately before was a condemnation of the rich who relied on wealth for their security and who used their position to oppress the needy. James describes rich people as pursuing a life of luxury and wanton pleasure. He was criticizing a heart-orientation toward self, a drive to live in selfish indulgence at the expense of others. He likens the rich person's heart to a calf being fattened for slaughter. James then points his readers toward the righteous alternative to the false solutions of wealth and earthly power: being "patient...until the coming of the Lord."

The Greek word translated as "patient" in 5:7 means more than waiting. We can all wait when we have no choice. James calls Christians to a gracious attitude while waiting, which is far more difficult. The Greek word translated here as "patience" is *makro-thumos*, describing a "restraint which does not hastily retaliate a wrong."[50] True patience does not produce bitterness, envy, or a desire for retribution.

James also points his readers to the object of their patience. They're not waiting to become rich and powerful on this earth; they're waiting for the coming of the Lord. If we Christians today could do this one thing—to live with a hopeful expectation of Jesus, so that his presence and the establishment of his kingdom were our consuming ambition—the church would be far more effective in bringing salt and light to this dark world. Instead, our hopes are often indistinguishable from the world, which pursues a life full of fleshly pleasure, with minimal suffering and little thought for eternal things.

James provides the farmer as an everyday example of patience. "The farmer waits for the precious produce of the soil, being patient about it, until it gets the early and late rains." James isn't talking about recreational gardeners. Many of us try to grow grass, flowers, and maybe a few vegetables, and we're grateful when they receive rain. But the farmer of ancient times relied on his crops to feed himself and his family. Rain wasn't merely nice to have; it was essential for survival. The soil's produce was precious indeed.

The farmer is an excellent example for us because farmers work extremely hard. They till, plow, plant, and prepare. They weed, guard, and protect. But they don't control the rain, and without water their crops will fail. Still today, a drought can be devastating to the most technologically advanced society. We still need rain, and only God can give it.

As Christians, we're called to labor in the fields of God's kingdom, but only God can create the fruit. Many aspects of a plant's gestation are mysterious, almost magical in their complexity. God is the orchestrator of it all. No matter how hard the farmer works, he's still dependent on the benevolence of his Creator. The farmer can do nothing to prompt the early and late rains, other than being patient and trusting the goodness of his God to provide.

The patience of the farmer doesn't suggest inaction or passivity. He must still till, sow, weed, and keep the pests away. But for the essential rain, he must wait. So too, we in this age have much to do in Christ's kingdom—to love and serve one another, to spread the gospel, and to be salt and light on this earth. But for ultimate things—the transformation of hearts and the salvation of sinners—we must wait on our Creator. And we must wait patiently, not growing in bitterness, not giving up out of frustration or exhaustion, and not succumbing to hatred for the very people we're called to minister to. As Paul wrote in Galatians:

> Let us not lose heart in doing good, for in due time we will reap if we do not grow weary. So then, while we have opportunity, let us do good to all people, and especially to those who are of the household of the faith. (Galatians 6:9-10)

James says we should be patient, like the farmer. We should strengthen our hearts, because the coming of the Lord is near. I'm reminded of Hosea's exhortation:

> So let us know, let us press on to know the Lord.
> His going forth is as certain as the dawn
> And He will come to us like the rain
> Like the spring rain watering the earth. (Hosea 6:3)

Christ's coming is certain. It's also imminent, although you might question that. We've been waiting nearly two thousand years, and he hasn't come yet. James's audience was waiting on Jesus to return, but they died without seeing it, as have the many generations of Christians since. So how practical is it to live with this hope?

As one commentator on the passage notes, "Anything that must happen [at some point], and could happen today, is in a very legitimate sense *at hand*."[51] We're called to anticipate his coming not because it will necessarily occur in our lifetime, but because his coming is inevitable, and we're to live as though it may happen at any moment.

Christ spoke of his return and told his disciples to be ready for it. Jesus spoke many parables with this theme, including those about the virgins and the lamps (Matthew 25:1-13), the doorkeeper (Luke 12:25-26; Mark 13:33-37), the house owner (Luke 12:39-40; Matthew 24:42-44), the servant in charge of the household (Matthew 24:45-51; Luke 12:41-46), and the talents (Matthew 25:14-30; Luke 19:11-27). In each of these parables, Christ teaches that his coming will be a surprise, and that we're to be ready. This means we're to live as though his return may happen at any moment. This perspective produces a joyous outcome, because holding Christ's return as our highest expectation fuels our hearts with a proper hope that displaces the false hopes of the world. To long for Christ's return is to remember our first love.

In 5:9, James shifts to relationships among believers: "Do not complain, brethren, against one another." At just the moment believers should be loving and supporting one another in the midst of challenging times, they often turn on each other. I see this today. The culture has grown very uncomfortable for followers of Jesus. The popular culture and shared values of this country are no longer safe waters in which to swim. Many American Christians feel politically disenfranchised, with both major political parties holding to positions inconsistent with their faith. Rather than being patient with one another amid our frustration and discomfort, we turn on one other. Christians are harsh with one another, criticizing one another. We all struggle with fear and discomfort, and in the midst of that stress we sometimes turn on the people we're closest with (just as often happens inside a family). We're so scared and frustrated, we feel like we have to turn on someone—and other Christians are the safest targets.

James calls us to an opposite approach. We're to love one another, encourage one another, and serve one another. We're all trying to figure out how to navigate this new culture, and none of us is getting it exactly right, so let's be gracious to one another. We do well to remember this exhortation from Paul:

> Therefore I, the prisoner of the Lord, implore you to walk in a manner worthy of the calling with which you have been called, with all humility and gentleness, with patience, showing tolerance for one another in love, being diligent to preserve the unity of the Spirit in the bond of peace. (Ephesians 4:1-3)

In the midst of today's cultural transformation, you may be thinking, "Is anyone else seeing this? Am I the only one who thinks the world has gone absolutely insane? Is anyone going to do anything about this?" You're not alone, but in this we must all be patient. As James points out in the last clause of 5:9, "Behold, the Judge is standing right at the door." Jesus will judge the deeds of men, and only Jesus is the judge.

> When the Son of Man comes in his glory and all his angels are with him, he will sit on his glorious throne. The people of every nation will be gathered in front of him. He will separate them as a shepherd separates the sheep from the goats. He will put the sheep on his right but the goats on his left. (Matthew 25:31-32)

We must be patient for Jesus's righteous judgment. God desires for many to enter his kingdom before that judgment comes, and we should cultivate the same desire in our heart—for the lost to be saved from that judgment. This was the heart of Christ toward us while we were still lost, and this is the inclination of heart we should show the world.

His judgment will come. Wrongs will be set right, and God will manifest his holiness. It's not our job to judge the eternal destination of the people we encounter or to avenge their wrongdoing. Our job is to be patient until Christ's return, because he will be the judge, and he will have the vengeance (Romans 12:19).

For those who've chosen to believe him and to receive his gift, Jesus Christ has absorbed this wrath in our stead. For those who reject him, a terrible reckoning will come. Every knee will bow and every tongue will confess (Philippians 2:10-11), but it's God who accomplishes this. Our job is to be patient, which requires deep belief and trust.

Life on this earth isn't comfortable for us, and it shouldn't be. We're strangers and aliens here, and this is not our home. Perhaps we've been too comfortable, but increasingly we're being forced to choose between comfort or the life to which God has called us.

The day is coming when all will be set right. Until then, God calls us to be patient, to love one another, tolerate one another, and look forward to Christ's imminent return.

Discussion Questions

1. We've seen that holding Christ's return as our highest expectation fuels our hearts with a proper hope, one that displaces the false hopes of the world. How is longing for Christ's return an important part of remembering our "first love"?
2. In what ways is the metaphor of the farmer a good description of living the Christian life?
3. What are some resources we tend to rely upon in place of God?

4. Review Paul's words in Ephesians 4:1-3, as an opposite approach to judging and criticizing and turning on one another. How can we go about growing in humility?

5. Does it seem strange to you that Christians have always been called to live ready for Christ's return, yet so far it hasn't happened in anyone's lifetime? How do we make sense of this?

26

EXAMPLES
OF ENDURANCE

As an example, brethren, of suffering and patience,
take the prophets who spoke in the name of the Lord.
We count those blessed who endured.
You have heard of the endurance of Job
and have seen the outcome of the Lord's dealings,
that the Lord is full of compassion and is merciful.
But above all, my brethren, do not swear,
either by heaven or by earth or with any other oath;
but your yes is to be yes, and your no, no,
so that you may not fall under judgment.

JAMES 5:10-12

As we encounter trials, it's both helpful and encouraging to
look to people who've successfully endured similar challenges. When we grieve, we gravitate to people who've
suffered a similar loss. When we encounter difficulties in raising children, we seek parents who navigated the same challenges.
When we suffer the fear accompanying a job loss, we talk with
someone else who made it through that frightening experience.

In 5:10-12, James exhorts his readers by pointing them toward the Old Testament prophets, who'd suffered as they were suffering. James wanted his readers to imitate the prophets by bearing their own suffering with patience, so they receive the blessings that come from faithful endurance.

Most of us would like to imitate the prophets in receiving a direct word from God, but few of us would choose the suffering life of an Old Testament prophet. God called these men to speak unpopular words to powerful people. Many Christians think that if they live in obedience to God, their life should be free from suffering. In fact, many see suffering as evidence of disobedience. But the prophets suffered *because* they faithfully presented the word of God, not in spite of it. They were often ridiculed, sometimes beaten, and almost always rejected. Some paid with their very lives.

Isaiah called his people to repentance to little effect, so he had to announce the coming judgment of his beloved homeland. Isaiah, for his faithfulness, was killed by being sawn in two. Jeremiah prophesied during one of the most painful seasons in Judah's history. He warned his countrymen about a coming judgment, and for his alleged lack of patriotism he suffered plots against his life, beatings, and imprisonment. When he complained to God regarding his treatment, God told him it would get worse (Jeremiah 12:5). Jewish tradition holds that he died in Egypt, where his exiled countrymen stoned him.[52] In obedience to God's command, Hosea married a harlot who served as an example of Israel's infidelity to God. He suffered the public humiliation of her unfaithfulness in order to advance God's message to his people. These are just some of the sufferings of God's faithful prophets.

These men suffered, and in their suffering they were examples of faithful endurance. In the midst of their suffering, they were true to God's word. They continued to obey God's instruction and to rebuke people who were ungrateful and hostile. The prophets rarely saw the fruit of repentance. They often saw the fearful reckoning that came when people rejected God's words. James called his readers to a similar faithful endurance in the midst of trial. He knew that in the midst of suffering, it's tempting to believe that God isn't good or that he has forsaken us. When we're in pain, it's hard to believe there's a divine plan behind it, or a coming reward.

From what we know of the personal histories of the prophets, few of them met peaceful ends, and none had easy lives. They suffered. Does this mean they were unloved, that God was not good, or that they were forsaken? No. In fact, James and his readers counted them blessed.

The writer of Hebrews helps us understand why the Jewish people considered the prophets blessed. He includes the "prophets of old" in a list of notable people "who by faith conquered kingdoms, performed acts of righteousness, obtained promises, shut the mouths of lions, quenched the power of fire, escaped from the edge of the sword, from weakness were made strong, became mighty in war, put foreign armies to flight" (Hebrews 11:33-34). The prophets had the distinctive experience of receiving a direct word from God and carrying out God's plans in a significant way. They were intimately acquainted with God and chosen by God to serve an important role in his kingdom.

After describing the victorious accomplishments of the prophets of old, the writer of Hebrews pivots to their suffering; he says they were "tortured, not accepting their release, so that they might obtain a better resurrection; and others experienced mockings and scourgings, yes, also chains and imprisonment. They were stoned, they were sawn in two, they were tempted, they were put to death with the sword; they went about in sheepskins and goatskins, being destitute, afflicted, ill-treated" (11:35-37). He goes on to say that although these faithful people gained divine approval through their faith, on this earth they didn't receive their promised reward (11:39).

What allowed the prophets to endure their trials faithfully, in spite of not receiving the promised things? They considered themselves strangers and aliens on this earth and desired a better country, a heavenly one (11:14-15). They were looking forward to the kingdom that cannot be shaken (12:26-27). Likewise for us: to patiently endure suffering on this earth, it's essential that we believe our sufferings in this present life cannot compare to the glories that will one day be revealed to us (Romans 8:18).

Socially conscious Christians emphasize the current physical needs of the poor. We should all be engaged in meeting those needs, because God calls us to do so. Unfortunately, it's also fashionable among some socially conscious Christians to elevate the priority of physical needs above spiritual needs, which is to elevate the present, shakable kingdom above the unshakable kingdom to come. Some consider it nobler to fill a man's stomach than to teach him about Jesus and his kingdom to come. But it's myopic to fill a man's stomach without pointing him to the eternal kingdom.

The reason we Christians often fail to boldly declare the eternal kingdom is that we don't believe in it, not really. We're practical atheists. We believe that what we can see is all there is. What comes after this earthly life is little more than an abstraction, a wish, a fairy tale. This wasn't true of the prophets.

The faith of many Christians is little more than a low-cost hedge against eternity that makes little practical difference in their day-to-day lives. In contrast, the prophets placed all their bets on the eternal kingdom. That is true faith, and without faith it's impossible to please God, no matter how many stomachs we fill (Hebrews 11:6).

In a society where earthly comforts abound, and the promised life of ease, rest, and luxury seems attainable with just a little more luck and effort, the promise of an eternal kingdom doesn't always appeal to us. But God's word calls us to focus our hope on that eternal kingdom. Peter writes, "Fix your hope completely on the grace to be brought to you at the revelation of Jesus Christ" (1 Peter 1:13). Paul writes, "For in hope we have been saved, but hope that is seen is not hope, for who hopes for what he already sees? But if we hope for what we do not see with perseverance we wait eagerly for it." (Romans 8:24).

To endure patiently in the midst of suffering, we must stop fixing our hope on earthly comforts and instead fix it completely on the greater kingdom to come. Suffering purifies our hope, because suffering reminds us that the highest and best we can hope for isn't found in the fleeting things of this earth. Patient endurance through suffering produces the spiritual grit that characterizes the for-real Christian.

This is not to say God is callous toward our current needs for either physical relief or emotional comfort. James writes that the Lord is full of compassion and is merciful. Jesus said our heavenly Father knows what we need even before we ask him, and he will clothe and feed us (Matthew 6:25-34). Paul writes that God will provide all our needs according to his riches in glory (Philippians 4:19), and that he comforts us in our troubles (1 Corinthians 1:3). But the meeting of our current needs is not an end in itself; it's not an ultimate thing.

Job's fortunes were restored twofold after his suffering, and he died an old man and full of days. We shouldn't expect all our suffering to be remedied on this earth, or all our losses to be restored, but Job's restoration is an example of God's compassion and a foreshadowing of the lavish blessings to come as a reward for our endurance.

The prophets suffered because they spoke in the name of the Lord. In 5:12, James criticizes people who through their oath-swearing are evidencing impatience and a desire to avoid suffering. In the Sermon on the Mount, Jesus said:

> But I say to you, make no oath at all, either by heaven, for it is the throne of God, or by the earth, for it is the footstool of his feet, or by Jerusalem, for it is the city of the great king. Nor shall you make an oath by your head, for you cannot make one hair white or black. But let your statement be, 'Yes, yes' or 'No, no'; anything beyond these is of evil. (Matthew 5:33-37)

To the modern ear, these teachings seem odd. Why does James say "*Above all*...do not swear"? Why was this issue of swearing so important to Jesus? Neither James nor Jesus had in mind here foul language, or what we might call "cussing." They were addressing the swearing of oaths. Today, when someone's accused of lying, he might say, "I swear on my mother's grave" or "I swear on the lives of my children" in order to buttress their credibility. People who resort to such oaths are often practiced liars, and they use these oaths to escape the consequences of the truth.

James is contrasting the prophets, who suffered for speaking the truth, with people who lie in order to avoid the suffering that comes from speaking the truth. In a time of persecution, these lies might include disavowals of the faith with clever false oaths. How often do we lie in order to escape undesirable consequences?

A lying tongue is among six things Solomon lists that God hates (Proverbs 6:17). We may think Scripture exaggerates the importance of false oaths, but we come to Scripture to be changed by it, not to judge it. What's important to God should be important to us. Let your yes be yes, and let your no be no. Suffer the consequences of a difficult truth rather than escaping difficulty with a convenient lie.

The life of a Christian on this earth will include suffering. Jesus promised this (John 16:33; Matthew 10:22). Despite this promise, suffering surprises us. We often interpret suffering as judgment, or as evidence that there's no God, or as proof that God isn't good. Earthly comfort entices us. Because comfort seems attainable, and because we convince ourselves that most people around us have attained it, we fix our hopes on that comfort rather than on future glories. We avoid suffering at all costs, including loss of our integrity and denial of our faith. We should instead imitate the prophets who patiently endured their suffering in the midst of service to God and so received great and eternal blessings.

A life of faith is a life of patient endurance amid suffering, where the hope in God's eternal kingdom displaces our hope in the fleeting pleasures of this earth.

Discussion Questions:

1. In biblical times, God would use the hunger of a famine to get people's attention. What kind of famine or hunger can God produce in our lives today to get our attention?
2. As a descriptive synomym for perseverance, what does "spiritual grit" mean to you?
3. Which is more difficult for you to experience in spiritual growth: development of a godly attribute, or elimination of a sinful behavior? Why so?

4. In Ephesians 2:10 we're called "to do good works which God prepared in advance for us to do." Many of these good works are God-sized tasks that require spiritual growth before we can complete them. Does that make you scared—or excited? Why so?

27

PRAY

Is anyone among you suffering? Then he must pray.
Is anyone cheerful? He is to sing praises.
Is anyone among you sick?
Then he must call for the elders of the church
and they are to pray over him, anointing him
with oil in the name of the Lord;
and the prayer offered in faith will restore the one who is sick,
and the Lord will raise him up,
and if he has committed sins, they will be forgiven him.
Therefore, confess your sins to one another,
and pray for one another so that you may be healed.

JAMES 5:13-16

*O*ne year when I was a young attorney, our biggest client's business was faltering. This created a great sense of insecurity in my firm because this one client constituted a high percentage of our total work. Losing this client would surely mean painful layoffs and pay cuts. We met in a strategy session to identify other client prospects, to create possible solutions for our current client, and to consider other options to keep us afloat. I asked my boss, "And what if none of those work?"

"Then," he said, "we pray."

He didn't say this because he believed in prayer, but to emphasize his hopelessness if our plans didn't work out.

His perspective on prayer is typical among modern western people. Prayer is the last resort of the hopeless, an act of utter desperation. We pray after we've exhausted every earthly resource. We don't pray because we believe in prayer's efficacy, but because we don't know what else to do. James calls us to a very different perspective. In all seasons, and in response to every circumstance, we're to pray.

James 5:13 says that we should pray if we're suffering. Our suffering comes in many forms. We suffer in our relationships, finances, health, and many other spheres of life. When faced with suffering, our first impulse is to muster our earthly resources in order to alleviate our suffering. James calls us to pray as a primary response, not as a final act of desperation.

James joins a chorus of other Bible writers in the call to pray. Paul wrote, "With all prayer and petition, pray at all times in the Spirit" (Ephesians 6:18), and, "Pray without ceasing" (1 Thessalonians 5:17). Peter also exhorts Christians to go to God first, "casting all of your anxieties on him, because he cares for you" (1 Peter 5:7). Luke says of Jesus, "He was telling them a parable to show that at all times they ought to pray and not to lose heart" (Luke 18:1).

Self-reliance stands high on the pedestal of earthly values, but God calls us to dependence on him. We resist prayer, in part, because prayer acknowledges our need for God, and we would rather rely on ourselves. Using prayer as a first response to suffering makes sense only if we believe in prayer's effectiveness, but most of us don't, not really. Consequently, our prayers are infrequent. When we do pray, we don't pray with fervency and belief, but as a hedge against the failure of our own efforts, which is where we're really placing our bets. Prayer should be the primary means by which we address suffering in our work, our physical condition, our marriages, our parenting, and every other facet of life.

James calls his readers to acknowledge God in their cheerfulness as well as in their suffering. Times of prosperity are perilous to spiritual health because in those seasons we can both fall in love with this world and cease to recognize our need for God in it. Prayers of gratitude and praise are effective antidotes to the perils of prosperity. When we thank God and praise God, we cultivate enduring contentment in him and ground our peace in a loving, unchanging God.

James specifically calls his readers to sing praises. It's not by accident or recent invention that we sing in church. God repeatedly calls us to sing (Psalms 33:1-3, 149:1-2; Ephesians 5:19; Colossians 3:16). Paul and Silas sang praises to God while they were in prison, exhibiting joyfulness and hope in the midst of their trial (Acts 16:25). Paul instructed us to "speak to one another in psalms and hymns and spiritual songs, singing and making melody with your heart to the Lord" (Ephesians 5:19). God himself models singing with delight when he tells us in Zephaniah 3:17 that he'll rejoice over his children with singing.

Singing praises is a form of prayer, a communication to God of our adoration for him. Singing true words about God's character directs our hearts toward him. You've probably experienced the delight of singing joyous praises to God. David wrote that when we take delight in God, he gives us the desires of our heart (Psalm 37:4). Worship is not a means to manipulate God into giving us what we want, but a discipline in which God aligns the desires of our heart with his great will for us. Do you feel stymied in this life, as if God is working in opposition to what you want to do? Then takes your eyes off your own plans, and regularly delight in the Lord through songs of praise. Replace the objects of your earthly ambitions with a desire for communion with God, and see if you don't find your path less obstructed and your life less frustrating.

James exhorts his readers, when they're sick, to seek prayer from the elders (5:14). Interestingly, he doesn't call his readers to pray for themselves when they're sick, but to seek prayer from the elders. The elders are to anoint the sick person with oil. There's a threefold promise with respect to this process: restoration, resurrection, and forgiveness. James says that the prayer offered in faith will restore the sick person, that the Lord will raise the sick person, and that if the sick person has sinned, he'll be forgiven.

Probably all of us have prayed for the sick, and many of us have seen church elders gather for anointing and prayer. Some of us have witnessed direct physical healing, but many of us have not. None of us has witnessed direct physical healing in response to every prayer. The only condition to God's promise of restoration is that the prayer be offered in faith. Misinterpretations of this passage have led to both false hope and false guilt. Some interpret this passage to mean that we're in control of our healing; if we have enough faith, then direct physical healing is assured. But even Paul prayed for healing that didn't come about (1 Corinthians 12:7-10). We'll all eventually succumb to illness, and we cannot avoid physical death altogether through faith. But grace through faith will deliver us from a second death, and not all restoration is physical. This passage promises restoration, resurrection, and forgiveness. We can be absolutely assured of these things in the eternal scope of God's kingdom.

I don't mean to imply that direct physical healing cannot or will not occur. There are abundant scriptural examples of direct physical healing, and many of us have witnessed or experienced similar healings today. There's no disease God cannot cure. And yet he often doesn't, for reasons that are sometimes invisible to us. But James's command remains. When we're sick, we should call for the elders to pray and anoint us, setting us apart to God, and he will restore, resurrect, and forgive as promised. As with most promises in Scripture, these promises will ring hollow unless we believe in an eternal life in the eternal kingdom.

James links sin and illness. In 5:15 he promises forgiveness for the ill, and in 5:16 he recommends confession as part of the healing process. He's echoing Christ's teaching. In Matthew we read the story of a paralytic who was brought to Jesus (Matthew 9:1-8). The friends of the paralytic broke through the roof of a crowded building and lowered their afflicted friend to Jesus. Matthew doesn't record their making a specific request, and I suspect they never made one. The need was obvious: the man needed healing. Jesus, however, offered something different: "Take courage, son; your sins are forgiven." This made people angry—possibly including the paralytic and his friends, though the only anger Matthew records is that of the religious teachers who thought Jesus was blasphemous for presuming to forgive sins.

In order to demonstrate his divinity and authority to forgive, Jesus healed the man after asking, "Which is easier to say, 'Your sins are forgiven,' or to say, 'Get up and walk?'" Scholars continue to argue over the right answer to that question, but the entire episode highlights a struggle we still have. We think our temporal, physical needs are more important than our spiritual health and eternal destination. Jesus addressed the bigger need first; he forgave the man his sins.

Sometimes we don't see direct responses to our prayers because we're asking for stones when Jesus wants to give us bread, and for snakes when he wants to give us fish (Matthew 7:9-10). God often addresses big needs in response to our small prayers, but rather than recognize the gift, we imitate the scribes by judging God for his failings, or we simply languish in confusion. All the while, Jesus is accomplishing the greater work.

There's sometimes a physical causation between our sin and our health—if we're gluttonous, or abuse alcohol or drugs, or commit sexual sin, or violate laws intended for our safety, then we suffer direct physical consequences. Sometimes there's a less direct relationship; anger and bitterness seem to metastasize in the physical organs. There's always a direct relationship between our sin and our spiritual health. James prescribes confession for all these ills, specifically confession to one another. Confessing silently to ourselves requires no faith and evidences no repentance. Outward confession to another—particularly to the one wronged—requires faith, and it's often the first step toward genuine repentance. Sin grows best in the dark, and as long as it's unconfessed, it will grow and will eventually enslave us. Confession is sometimes terrifying to contemplate. It's also the only way out from under consuming sin. Confess your sins to each other, and you'll be healed.

Throughout my life, I've prayed in the face of suffering. Sometimes prayer wasn't my first response, and I've often prayed with unbelief, but I've prayed because I had parents who taught me to pray. God has sometimes answered my prayers quickly, directly, and affirmatively. There are other long-uttered prayers that, in my limited perception, still await resolution. But God's answers have most often taken a different path than I would have expected. I prayed for a healthier marriage, and God called me to confess silent sin to my wife. The healthier marriage came only after suffering through the sorrow that followed. I prayed for more prosperity at work, and God used a long period of professional stagnancy to show me the idolatry I'd allowed to grow in my life, leading to confession and repentance. I prayed for a child's behavioral and academic issues, and God responded with the painful exposure of deeper sin, eventually leading to confession, repentance, and radical spiritual transformation.

In all those scenarios, I could have raised my fist at God and questioned his character for failing to answer my prayers. Sometimes I did. After all, I didn't pray for more suffering, I prayed for less. But I see more clearly now that I was asking God to move the pieces on my checkerboard, while God was operating as a three dimensional chess master. I see only in part now, but one day I will see fully, when I see him face to face (1 Corinthians 13:12).

Years ago, my firm was right to strategize and develop a plan when our client was struggling. But my first response and daily practice should have been prayer. Even as I worked to do what I could in service to my firm, I should have placed my true hope in the God who provides, not in the works of my own hands. As the situation progressed, I should have continued in prayer and kept my eye on what God was doing on a level higher than my immediately perceived need. Praying through our suffering takes us deeper into our relationship with God and our dependence on him. This increases our intimacy with Christ and our experience of resilient joy.

Discussion Questions:

1. Does prayer come easily to you, or is it difficult? What is your greatest obstacle in prayer?
2. What are your thoughts on prayers for healing? Have you ever participated in a ceremony where the elders have anointed a

sick person with oil as they prayed for him? What was the outcome, and how did it affect your perception of prayer?

3. Do you find it odd that James links healing with confession? Why do you think he does this? Have you ever experienced a connection between confession and healing in your life or seen it in others?

28

PRAY
EFFECTIVELY

The effective prayer of a righteous man can accomplish much.
Elijah was a man with a nature like ours, and he prayed earnestly
that it would not rain, and it did not rain on the earth for three
years and six months. Then he prayed again,
and the sky poured rain and the earth produced its fruit.

JAMES 5:16-20

When I was fourteen, I went on a summer-long mission trip to Jamaica. We were far away from the beach and spent our days under the hot sun, building a twelve-foot cinder block security wall around an orphanage in inner-city Kingston. While working, we were required to memorize daily Bible verses in the King James Version. We complained about this, but despite our resistance, we acquired a mental treasury of wonderful scriptures. Mixing concrete by hand while quoting those verses over and over forever etched those scriptures on my brain.

One of them is this verse: "Therefore, confess your sins to one another, and pray for one another, so that you may be healed.

The effectual fervent prayer of a righteous man availeth much" (James 5:16).

This is one of those verses that shows up on coffee mugs, Christian calendars, and inspirational Facebook posts. With the benefit of selective reading, the verse's message is straightforward: Confess, pray, be healed; prayer availeth much. But the in-between words make the verse more challenging.

Even as a fourteen-year-old, I struggled to derive encouragement from what James says here because of two concerns. First, the verse seems circular: Effectual prayer is effective. Well, of course, and I suppose the corollary is that ineffectual prayer is ineffective. How much of a promise is that, really? Second, the promise has a precondition I feel I can't satisfy: it's the prayer of a *righteous* man that availeth much. Am I righteous enough to satisfy the condition? If not, does the promise really mean anything?

Beyond these questions of scriptural interpretation, the greater issue that has plagued my prayer life is cynicism. I wonder whether prayer can really change anything. If God is sovereign, how can the prayers of one man alter his path? Isn't prayer a cop-out, an excuse not to work hard and do for myself? In darker seasons, I've asked whether God is there at all. If he's there, does he listen? If he listens, does he care?

I suspect most of us have asked similar questions, because a lot of us have been praying for many things, and many of those prayers seem to remain unanswered.

Because of these questions, and because life is busy and loud and because other spiritual disciplines are easier, our prayer lives are often insipid. My ambition is to stoke our passion for prayer and to address the cynicism that so often dampens our prayer lives.

What do we do with the apparent circularity of this promise about effective prayer accomplishing much? In this, the King

James translation is helpful. It speaks of "effectual fervent prayer," suggesting that there's more to the original Greek word than we get in the English word "effective." That Greek word is *energeo*, which means to be active and energetic.[53] This explains the presence of the word "fervent" in the KJV. The word "effective" here is describing not prayer's outcome, but its nature—which is to be energetic and fervent.

Does this mean we need to wave our arms or adopt an active physical posture in prayer? Scripture doesn't prescribe this elsewhere, and there's little description of the physical posture adopted by Christ and the apostles in their prayer lives. In fact, in Matthew, Jesus warns his followers against using "vain repetitions" or "babbling like pagans" in prayer (Matthew 6:7). So effectual prayer must be something other than mindless, albeit passionate repetition of words by rote.

What does fervent prayer look like? Jesus gave us a number of parables that help us understand what it means to be fervent in our prayers:

> Now he was telling them a parable to show that at all times they ought to pray and not to lose heart, saying, "In a certain city there was a judge who did not fear God and did not respect man. There was a widow in that city, and she kept coming to him, saying, 'Give me legal protection from my opponent.' For a while he was unwilling; but afterward he said to himself, 'Even though I do not fear God nor respect man, yet because this widow bothers me, I will give her legal protection, otherwise by continually coming she will wear me out.'" And the Lord said, "Hear what the unrighteous judge said; now, will not God bring about justice for his elect who cry to him day and night, and will he delay

long over them? I tell you that he will bring about justice for them quickly. However, when the Son of Man comes, will he find faith on the earth?" (Luke 18:1-8)

It happened that while Jesus was praying in a certain place, after he had finished, one of his disciples said to him, "Lord, teach us to pray just as John also taught his disciples." And he said to them, "When you pray, say: 'Father, hallowed be Your name. Your kingdom come. Give us each day our daily bread. And forgive us our sins, for we ourselves also forgive everyone who is indebted to us. And lead us not into temptation.'" Then he said to them, "Suppose one of you has a friend, and goes to him at midnight and says to him, 'Friend, lend me three loaves; for a friend of mine has come to me from a journey, and I have nothing to set before him' and from inside he answers and says, 'Do not bother me; the door has already been shut and my children and I are in bed; I cannot get up and give you anything.' I tell you, even though he will not get up and give him anything because he is his friend, yet because of his persistence he will get up and give him as much as he needs. So I say to you, ask, and it will be given to you; seek, and you will find; knock, and it will be opened to you. For everyone who asks, receives; and he who seeks, finds; and to him who knocks, it will be opened. Now suppose one of you fathers is asked by his son for a fish; he will not give him a snake instead of a fish, will he? Or if he is asked for an egg, he will not give him a scorpion, will he? If you then, being evil, know how to give good gifts to your children, how much more will your heavenly Father give the Holy Spirit to those who ask him?" (Luke 11:1-13)

In the same passage where Christ gave his disciples the model of the Lord's Prayer, he also emphasized the need for persistence in prayer. The unrighteous judge and the sleeping neighbor are examples of imperfect people who yielded to someone's persistence in granting a request. As Jesus's Sermon on the Mount indicates, our heavenly Father differs from these people in two critical respects. First, he is perfect (Matthew 5:48). Second, he gladly gives good gifts (Matthew 7:11). The purpose of these parables is to emphasize the necessity and value of persistence in our prayer.

Why must we be persistent? Why isn't it enough to simply ask? If these gifts are good and the Giver is good, why does he make us ask for them in the first place?

The answer is that God wants us to keep seeking him (Colossians 3:2). God desires that we acknowledge our dependence on him not because he needs our affirmation, but because he knows our natural tendency is to strive for independence and to deny our need for God. This natural tendency separates God's children from the good and perfect gifts the Father has to give.

This has been true since the garden of Eden. It's true today. We always need him, but we tend to seek him only when reminded that we need him. Suffering is what reminds us. By seeking independence, we deny ourselves the greatest gift of all, which is abiding in Christ—because in abiding lies significance, security, joy, and peace.

One of the most intimate perspectives we have on Christ and prayer comes from Christ's own earnest prayer in his darkest moment in the garden of Gethsemane:

And he came out and proceeded as was his custom to the Mount of Olives; and the disciples also followed him. When he arrived at the place, he said to them, "Pray that you may not enter into temptation." And he withdrew from them about a stone's throw, and he knelt down and began to pray, saying, "Father, if You are willing, remove this cup from Me; yet not My will, but Yours be done." Now an angel from heaven appeared to him, strengthening him. And being in agony he was praying very fervently; and his sweat became like drops of blood, falling down upon the ground. When he rose from prayer, he came to the disciples and found them sleeping from sorrow, and said to them, "Why are you sleeping? Get up and pray that you may not enter into temptation." (Luke 22:39-46)

This was effectual fervent prayer. Christ's prayer stood in contrast to the attitude of his disciples. They didn't know the gravity of the approaching events, but Jesus did. The disciples didn't truly believe in the effectiveness of prayer, but Jesus did. Do we have to sweat drops of blood for our prayer to be fervent? No, but in contrast to Jesus's example, my typical prayers are weak, distracted, and unbelieving. The narrative suggests that Christ was in prayer for hours. This prayer was not a quick send-up, an afterthought, or a hedge. This was desperate prayer, passionate prayer, persistent prayer.

We should note another critical fact about Jesus's prayer in Gethsemane—the Father did not grant Christ's request for the cup to be removed. Was Christ's prayer then ineffective? Although a ministering angel was sent to comfort Jesus in this time of dire need, the Father's plan for the redemption of the world was not to be undone in this moment of Christ's very human dread of the hours to come. A greater thing was at work, as Christ himself acknowledged in his prayer: "Yet not my will, but Your will be done." The mere fact that our prayers aren't immediately answered in the way we seek doesn't mean they're ineffective. At Gethsemane, the Father wasn't distant, nor was he hard-hearted. He was compassionate—both to his Son in that moment of weakness, and to all humanity in proceeding with his plan of redemption in the face of pain and adversity.

The effectual, fervent prayer to which James calls us is persistent prayer. It's prayer that flows from the combination of belief and need, and it accomplishes much. What it accomplishes is often different from what we expect—and better.

My second difficulty with James's promise concerning prayer is that it's conditioned on my righteousness, and I know I'm often horrifically unrighteous. The Bible teaches that Christ's righteousness is imputed to me (Romans 3:21-22; 10:3; 1 Corinthians 1:30; 2 Corinthians 5:21; Colossians 3:34), which sort of gets me over that hump. The wondrous gospel truth that a believer's salvation is attained through Christ's righteousness is unequivocal. But does that mean all calls to righteous living in Scripture are really masked references to our identity in Christ? If so, do those calls mean anything? If not, does James mean that only perfectly righteous people can expect to have their prayers answered?

The apostle John writes, "The one who practices righteousness is righteous, just as he is righteous; the one who practices sin is of the devil" (1 John 3:7). Though we're saved by grace through faith, there are still consequences to the way we live. When we're out of alignment with God's word and God's plan, we shouldn't have confident expectation of fulfilled prayer. If the promise of accomplishing much through prayer wasn't conditioned on righteousness, then the promise of answered prayer would not be comforting, but monstrous.

We serve a righteous God who grants righteous requests, and we wouldn't want it to be otherwise. The word "righteous" describes a person who has measured his life not by his own standard, but by God's. Righteous people are rightly related to God, and they walk with God as a result of this relationship.[54] There's a synergy to this. As we walk with God and abide in Christ, our desires are in accord with his wishes and his Word. Our prayers are often answered because we're praying in a manner consistent with God's character and plan.

You might object: "But isn't the purpose of prayer to alter the course of things, to attain the things for which we're asking? If by walking in righteousness I'm naturally asking for things God already intends to give, is prayer really changing anything?" Of course something *is* changing; *you* are changing. The discipline of prayer isn't about learning to manipulate God to get what we want, but as in all good and godly things, it's about our being conformed to the image of Christ.

When we're rightly aligned with God, we'll experience frequent answers to prayer because we're praying in accordance with his character and his plan.

As if anticipating objections, James provides the example of Elijah—the man whose prayers stopped the rain. Though he was a mighty and righteous man of God, Elijah was imperfect and prone to melancholy and depression. He served in the northern kingdom of Israel where the unrighteous King Ahab had married the notoriously wicked queen Jezebel, who has come to represent wickedness for all time. Jezebel worshiped Baal, the greatest of pagan gods. Among other things, Baal was the god who produced crops. Elijah's prayer is implied rather than described in 1 Kings 17, but Elijah told King Ahab it wouldn't rain again until the prophet said otherwise. The rain stopped, the brooks dried up, and famine plagued the land—showing that Yahweh, not Baal, was the God who produced crops.

During the ensuing years of famine, some of the most notable stories from Elijah's ministry occurred. This was when Elijah blessed the widow of Zarephath with a bottomless jar of oil, which saw her and her son through the famine. This was also when Elijah confronted the prophets of Baal on Mount Carmel. Near the end of the famine, Elijah told King Ahab it was about to rain again, before there was any indication of rain.

Elijah then went on top of Mount Carmel and put his head between his knees. The image speaks of intense, fervent prayer. Elijah told his servant to go and look toward the sea, and the servant saw nothing. "Go back," he said. Elijah continued to pray. Seven times he told his servant, "Go back and look." On the seventh trip, the servant saw the hint of a cloud on the horizon. Elijah immediately sent the servant with a message for Ahab—start for home now before the storm stops you. Then the deluge came (1 Kings 18:41-46).

Why did Elijah have to send the servant seven times? Why did Naaman have to bathe seven times in the Jordan River to be healed of leprosy (1 Kings 5)? Why did Abraham have to wait twenty-five years for Isaac (Genesis 12–25)? Why did the Israelites have to march seven times around Jericho before its walls fell (Joshua 6)? Why did Jesus wait to go to Bethany until Lazarus had been dead for four days (John 11:39)? Why did Jesus have to lie three days in the tomb? Why does God make us wait for so long before he answers our prayers? It's because in the waiting, our obedience and persistence help to accomplish what God desires in us—our being conformed to the image of Christ.

The effectual fervent prayer of a person who's rightly aligned with God in their living and in their asking availeth much.

My favorite book on prayer is Paul Miller's *A Praying Life*. In that book, Miller identifies cynicism as our chief obstacle to a rich prayer life. Cynicism is the spirit of our age. We're cynical because our public figures have failed us, the world seems very angry, and we've asked God for too many things that never came to pass. Miller posits that cynics imagine they're on a quest for authenticity, and they feel superior because they think they see through everything. He writes,

> While purporting to "see through" others' facades, cynics lack purity of heart. A significant source of cynicism is the fracture between my heart and my behavior. It goes something like this: My heart gets out of tune with God, but life goes on. So I continue to perform and say Christian things, but they are just words. I talk about Jesus. There is a disconnect between what I present and who I am. My words sound phony too. In short, my empty religious performance leads me to think that everyone is phony. The very thing I am doing, I accuse others of doing. Adding judgment to hypocrisy breeds cynicism.[55]

Miller goes on to describe Christian cynics as double-minded, the term James uses in 1:7-8 to explain why certain people were not receiving answers to prayer. Miller then says:

> Cynicism looks in the wrong direction. It looks for the cracks in Christianity instead of looking for the presence of Jesus. It is an orientation of the heart. The...cure for cynicism, then, is this: develop an eye for Jesus.[56]

Are we looking for the cracks or for the presence? When we receive an answer to prayer, we might say cynically, "Well, honestly, that was probably going to happen anyway." Or we might say, "It happened, but not in the way I wanted." Or, "I prayed for three things; one happened, another sort of happened, the third didn't happen at all. So I don't know what to think." Or—we might rejoice in gratitude and amazement at God's goodness.

Train your eyes to see the beauty of Christ's working in your life, in ways long and short, big and small, subtle and overt. Choose to hang around with people who've cultivated this skill and who can help point your eye toward the beauty of God's working. How much joy do we forfeit because we haven't trained our eyes to see Jesus?

Find a group of like-minded people who'll pray earnestly and fervently for each other. Don't surrender to the cynical fatalism that believes prayer doesn't matter, or that it's little more than a personal therapy session. Pray like it matters. Be persistent.

As you continue to meet and pray with others, encourage one other with what God is doing. This is one of the reasons God calls us to gather together, and in doing this, you'll train your eyes to see Jesus.

Discussion Questions

1. What do you think fervent prayer is like? How could your prayer life become more fervent?
2. Is it discouraging for you to think your prayer's outcome might be to change your heart rather than your circumstances?
3. Has cynicism dampened your enthusiasm for prayer? How can we battle the influence of cynicism in our spiritual lives?

AFTERWORD

My brethren, if any among you strays from the truth
and one turns him back, let him know that he who
turns a sinner from the error of his way will save
his soul from death and will cover a multitude of sins.

JAMES 5:20

After staring into the mirror of James's epistle, you might ask yourself now, "Am I really a Christian?" If you've never embraced the truth, or have strayed from it, this is a healthy question to ask. But note that James isn't calling us from fleshly failure toward fleshly performance, but from error to truth.

In 5:20, James is still addressing his "brethren"; these are churchgoing people. But some have strayed from the truth and are living in error. They're destined for death.

The truth to which James directs these sinners is the good news, the gospel of the Lord Jesus Christ, the law of liberty. This gospel covers over a multitude of sins. As Paul writes,

The Law came in so that the transgression would increase;
but where sin increased, grace abounded all the more, so

that, as sin reigned in death, even so grace would reign through righteousness to eternal life through Jesus Christ our Lord. (Romans 5:20-21)

God's grace extends to Christians because God gives it, not because Christians earn it. To be a Christian is to believe not in a man who was a notable ethical teacher two thousand years ago, but in Jesus Christ, the Son of God, who was crucified and raised from the dead and who now lives and reigns in heaven. In return for this belief, Christians receive eternal life.

This eternal life doesn't begin with our earthly death, but with our belief in the risen Jesus. As Christ himself said, the kingdom of God is in our midst even now (Luke 17:21). When Jesus announced this kingdom, he invited his followers to enter through repentance and belief (Mark 1:15). Because this life begins now, it should look different now. This is the transformed life James describes in his letter.

Suffering often serves to expose our unbelief, our false gods, and our unconfessed sin. In this, suffering is a mercy, because momentary affliction can deliver us from a greater eternal peril or from a spiritually tepid life. My prayer is that this book will be useful in helping you to view your suffering anew, and to shift you from bitterness and fear to faithful endurance—because in that process lies joy and the abundant life.

The most painful and difficult seasons of my life are always—always—the most useful in my ministry to others. I embrace every hurt, every disappointment and every every confession of sin because it's in those moments I've known most closely the real power of God. (My journal entry for June 8, 2017)

ACKNOWLEDGMENTS

This book began as a compilation of lessons I prepared for the Journey Sunday School Class at Church of the Apostles in Atlanta. It has been a privilege to teach wonderful groups of deep, committed, passionate, for-real Christians for more than seventeen years. Knowing that such a group awaits valuable biblical instruction every week has kept me on my toes and forced me deeper into God's word. I'm indebted to that group for giving me the teacher's podium.

I especially want to thank our church's director of small groups, T. J. Diamond, who faithfully leads the Journey Class and suggested that I prepare a book based on my talks. This book would not have existed without that encouragement. T. J., a gifted preparer of provocative questions, also prepared the discussion questions at the end of each chapter.

I naively believed it would be a small matter to turn those written lectures into book chapters, but that process took quite a bit of work, becoming indeed a team effort. I've had a number of readers helping me, including T. J., my neighbor Kevin Loechl, my fellow Apostles member (and occasional co-teacher) David Nutter, and editor Thomas Womack. Kevin has walked many miles by my side and given me the privilege of insight into his own suffering. David is a man of deep, active faith, and he never lets me off the hook. He has offered a number of challenging and helpful insights that changed some of the passages in this book.

I also owe a great deal of thanks to my bride Toria. She has been a tremendous support and help as I've written this book, unwavering in her encouragement. This is true not just regarding the book, but throughout the trials of our married life, many of which I mention in this book. She's unconcerned with appearances, and seeks to live a fully integrated life of faith. Above all, she loves Jesus, and her countenance radiates his presence in her life.

I also thank my children Jack, Mary Kate, Will, and Grace Anne, each of whom has contributed in some way to this book. Watching them mature has given me great insight into the nature of God and his work.

ABOUT THE AUTHOR

Stephen D. Peterson was born to Scandinavian stock in St. Paul, Minnesota, and after an itinerant childhood (including stops in Pennsylvania, Texas, Georgia, Tennessee, and Idaho), settled in a suburb of Atlanta. In between, he studied at King University and the Emory University School of Law. He's a practicing lawyer and adult Sunday school teacher at Church of the Apostles in Atlanta, where he has been a member throughout his adult life. Steve and Toria have four children.

NOTES

1   Flavius Josephus, *Antiquities of the Jews, book XX, ch. 9.*

2   John MacArthur, *The MacArthur Bible Commentary*, (Nashville: Thomas Nelson, 2005), 1879.

3   Spiros Zodhiates, "Lexical Aids to the New Testament," in *The Complete Word Study Dictionary: New Testament* (Chattanooga, Tennessee: AMG Publishers, 1992, rev. ed. 1993), entry for "3956 *pás.*"

4   *Zondervan NASB Study Bible* (Grand Rapids, Michigan: Zondervan, 1999), 1805.

5   Zodhiates, entry for "5046 *téleios.*"

6   Zodhiates, entry for "3648 *holóklēros.*"

7   W. E. Vine, *Expository Dictionary of New Testament Words* (Old Tappan, New Jersey: Revell, 1940), entry for "Wisdom: 1. *sophia.*"

8   *MacArthur Bible Commentary*, 1882.

9   Zodhiates, entry for "4678 *sophía.*"

10 Constable, Thomas L., "Notes on James" (2012), 10.

11 Vine, entry for "Humble: (A)1. *taipenos.*"

12 Vine, entry for "Glory: (A)1. *kauchaomai.*"

13 *MacArthur Bible Commentary*, 1882.

14 Tim Kizziar, as quoted in Francis Chan, *Crazy Love* (Colorado Springs: David C. Cook, 2008), 93.

15 *MacArthur Bible Commentary*, 1883.

16 Proverbs 23:20-21; 28:7; 23:2; 2 Peter 1:5-7; 2 Timothy 3:1-9; 2 Corinthians 10:5.

17 Compare Psalm 136:7.

18 As in Hebrews 6:11.

19 *Zondervan NASB Study Bible*, 1805.

20 Vine, entry for "Religion: 1. *Thrēskia*" and for "Religious: *thrēskos.*"

21 Zodhiates, entry for "1980 *episképtomai.*"

22 http://www.gallup.com/poll/159548/identify-christian.aspx.

23 *MacArthur Bible Commentary*, 1885.

24 *MacArthur Bible Commentary*, 1885.

25 Zodhiates, entry for "3551 *nómos.*"

26 I have my son's express permission to tell this story.

27 From Luther's preface to his translation of the New Testament in September 1522.

28 *MacArthur Bible Commentary*, 1885.

29 *MacArthur Bible Commentary*, 1885.

30 *MacArthur Bible Commentary*, 1885.

31 *The Wiersbe Bible Commentary: New Testament* (Colorado Springs: David C. Cook, 2007), 860.

32 All these commands are found in the Sermon on the Mount, Matthew 5–7.

33 See *MacArthur Bible Commentary*, 1889; Constable, 39.

34 Philip Schaff, *History of the Christian Church, vol. I, Apostolic Christianity*, rev. ed. (New York: Scribner's Sons, 1910), 212-213.

35 "Webster's Dictionary 1828—Online Edition," Noah Webster, *American Dictionary of the English Language*; http://webstersdictionary1828.com/Dictionary/wisdom.

36 Vine, note for entry on "Wisdom."

37 James Strong, *A Concise Dictionary of the Words in the Greek New Testament*, entry for "1990 *epistémon.*"

38 Vine, entry for "Meekness: (B)1. *prautēs.*"

39 Zodhiates, entry for "4240 *praútēs.*"

40 Zodhiates, entry for "53 *hagnós.*"

41 Strong, *Concise Dictionary*, entry for "1933 *epieikēs.*"

42 The word translated as "reasonable" (NASB) is rendered in the King James Version as "easy to be entreated."

43 Zodhiates, entry for "1656 éleos."

44 Zodhiates, entry for "505 *anupókritos.*"

NOTES

45 Zodhiates, entries for "4171 *pólemos*" and "3163 *máchē.*"

46 Strong, *Concise Dictionary*, entry for "2237 *hēdonē.*"

47 This includes verses like John 14:14, where Jesus said, "If you ask me for anything in my name, I will do it."

48 R. J. Zwi Warblowsky and G. Wigoder, eds., *Oxford Dictionary of the Jewish Religion* (New York: Oxford University Press, 1997), entry for "betrothal."

49 Watchman Nee, *Sit, Walk, Stand* (Carol Stream, Illinois: Tyndale House Publishers, 1977).

50 *The Sunday School Journal*, vol. 35 (1901), 426.

51 Zane Hodges, *The Epistle of James* (Nashville: Thomas Nelson, 1994), 111.

52 https://www.britannica.com/biography/Jeremiah-Hebrew-prophet.

53 Zodhiates, entry for "1754 *energéō.*"

54 Zodhiates, entry for "1342 *díkaios.*"

55 Paul Miller, *A Praying Life* (Colorado Springs: NavPress, 2009), 92.

56 Miller, 96.

Learn more about Stephen Peterson's thoughts

on "For Real" faith at

ForRealChrisitian.com